POCKET LIBRARY OF STUDIES IN ART
—— XXVII ——

RICHARD FREMANTLE

GOD AND MONEY
FLORENCE AND THE MEDICI IN THE RENAISSANCE

Including
Cosimo I's Uffizi
and its Collections

LEO S. OLSCHKI EDITORE
1992

Many thanks to the Gabinetto Fotografico of the Soprintendenza alle Belle Arti in Florence, and to Antonio Quattrone, for permission to publish photographs. Thanks also to Prof. Antonio Paolucci, and to Luisa Palli.

Cover Illustration: *Clock Face*, by Paolo Uccello (Paolo di Dono), c.1443. Florence, Cathedral.

ISBN 88 222 3939 3

The address of the publisher, Leo S. Olschki is:
Viuzzo del Pozzetto 8 (Viale Europa), 50126 Firenze, Italia.
E-mail= celso@olschki.it. Web= htlp://www.olschki.it.
Tel: 0039 055 653 0684. Fax: 0039 055 653 0214.

Reprinted 1997 & 2001. Minor additions and revisions have been made for the third printing, and a short Bibiography has been added.

for Janet Hobhouse

TABLE OF CONTENTS

PREFACE

Florence: The World's Museum of the Renaissance

What was the "Renaissance", or "rinascita" as the Italians call it – the great movement of history which began as the Middle Ages ended?

I. *The Renaissance and Christianity*

In its broadest outlines the Renaissance sprang from a long, slow rebellion against the kind of life which had existed during the Middle Ages, and the Christian Church government which greatly controlled that life. Instead of an attempt to reform the Church, as were earlier protests, the Renaissance began as a secular detachment from Church authority, a lay reform of ordinary, everyday Christian life. It continued and blossomed as a cultural movement and a period of transition, across the whole of Europe. All aspects of life were reformed to adapt to the new liberal attitude towards the Papacy, and to the growing interest in Nature and in Man which displaced the slowly waning interest in Christianity.

At the beginning of the Renaissance Europe was still dominated by the Christian religion and by Christian ideas. By its end religion and Christianity had become dominated by trade, science, and civil politics.

The Papacy, that is the Church government at Rome, of course resisted the reforming movement of the Renaissance, and was itself changed by this resistance. It, too was secularized, slowly becoming a great patron of the new liberal forms, attempting to take back the leadership of the new lay-oriented Christianity.

For centuries before the Renaissance, every European's vision of life had been filled with Christian objects, Christian rituals, Christian laws.

Christianity wasn't just a religion. For over a thousand years – from about 300 AD until after 1300 AD – it was the one universal government in Europe. It had a central bureaucracy in Rome, an organization with priests and churchs spread to every village and hamlet in Europe, its own taxes, and its own universal language, Latin. The Church oversaw birth, education, marriage or holy orders, all professional activity, the education of children, sickness, old age, death, burial, and of course, in general, society's morals. All the things that civil governments do today, the Church did then. Regardless of who was the local ruler, or what language he spoke, Europe's one enduring government was the Christian Church with its center at Rome.

There are moments in the Renaissance when the rebellion against Church government also included rebellion against some aspect of Christ's teaching. But these were mostly minor, and usually traceable to the Church's interpretation of that teaching. On the whole it was not Christ's way of life or his invitation to charity and love of one's enemy, which caused the rebellion, but the Church's own view of life, and Church laws.

The Renaissance began during the late 14th and early 15th centuries, in a spiritual rebellion against the Papacy, and that revolt continued to be a catalyst throughout its long development. The rebellion pulled in elements which became the most integral and wonderful parts of the Renaissance, as people sought to replace belief in the Church's teaching with other beliefs. The Renaissance became in fact an Age of Search.

At the beginning of the Renaissance there was an attempt to see Christ and Christianity in a new, personal, humanistic way, an attempt on the part of Christians to be more spiritual in the face of a Christian Papacy which no longer acted very spiritually. With this came a deep study of earlier history and literature, particularly that of pre-Christian Rome and of ancient Greece, as well as the study of every aspect of nature, of economics, of government, of the rights of man, and of all other facets of man's natural existence. All this developed and replaced the previous interest in Christianity.

The word Renaissance means "re-birth". In the sense that they hadn't been generally studied for themselves since pre-Christian times, these new interests did create a re-birth. They produced new forms in painting, sculpture and architecture, new forms of music and theatre, in dress, in household furnishings, in speech, in thought, and above all, in beliefs.

2. The Renaissance and Man

The great beauty of the Renaissance comes from human-beings seeing everything in nature as a developing beauty, and from seeing themselves, particularly their own minds, as an integral part of that beauty, if not its center. Christ on the cross, during the Renaissance, ceased to be a symbol of a distant, omnipotent God, and became an ordinary suffering, but triumphant human being. Men and women, in a converse sense, remained the ordinary human beings of the Middle Ages – Christians – but became at the same time, God and Goddesses of nature.

The beauty of the Renaissance is also to do with movement, for beauty and change are intertwined, different expressions of the same force. The Renaissance was a time of great movement, as people searched about their physical and spiritual environment for new knowledge and new laws to re-place those of the old Mediaeval God. Prince Henry the Navigator explored the coasts of Africa. Vasco da Gama sailed around that continent to the Far East. Columbus crossed the Atlantic to the New World. Magellan sailed right round the whole Earth. These are only indicators of all the movement and discovery – both physical as well as in the realm of ideas – of the Renaissance. Europeans fanned out across the globe, while likewise entering into every particle of matter and idea, to search for new truths. Painting in particu-lar – that is, pictures of people and of the world – became a great tool in this new search.

The Renaissance was also a great renewal of Man's spir-ituality, but one which took place outside the mediaeval forms of life.

3. The Renaissance and the Church: the Great Schism

From sometime before the year 1200, concurrent with an enormous growth in European population and wealth, a dis-comfort with the Christian death-oriented existence of medi-aeval Europe became evident everywhere. Attempts were made by many individual reformers – the most famous are Saints Francis (1182-1226) and Dominic (1170-1221) – to lead people back to a simpler, more Christian life. But these returns to an earlier spirit were mostly short-lived. By 1400 the discomfort was also being alleviated by an open search for new meanings to life.

These various attempts at reform became absorbed into everyday existence, changing Europe's view of Christianity, while creating a wish for ever greater changes.

Spurred by an event which sealed the tomb of mediaeval Christianity, a search for new realities in nature became Europeans' primary concern. Between 1378 and 1417 there appeared four lines of rival heads of the Christian government, four lines of Popes, each with his Cardinals, claiming spiritual legitimacy as heirs of St Peter, each claiming to be Christ's true, holy, representative on earth. This event is called the *Great Schism*. It followed upon a long period during which the Papacy had left a political and spiritual void in Italy by not residing at Rome, but at Avignon, in what is now the south of France. This absence, followed by the Schism, left Church government in such discredit and such disarray that Europeans took their future spiritual life, so to speak, into their own hands. Inquiry into the true nature of the world and of Man becomes their primary goal. Over the hundred years which followed the Schism, Christianity became ever more secondary, and ever more a personal matter.

Those hundred years of change, and of tension, between the growing secular State and the declining Papacy – from the end of the Schism in 1417, to Luther's open rebellion against the Papacy in 1517 and the beginning of the Protestant Reformation in northern Europe – are the years in which the Renaissance flowered in Florence. The old idols were dead. No new ones yet lived.

As the Renaissance began, the Great Schism ended at a Council, in Constance in southern Germany. During the Council the three existing Popes were all deposed, and a fourth was elected. This new Pope – Oddone Colonna, a Roman – took the name Martin V (1417-1431). He began at once to try to re-establish the Church's former authority in Rome as the ultimate source of law in Europe. But it was to be a losing battle.

Trade had been and continued to be the motor-force of the changes taking place in Europe. From the mid-11th century on, it was this trade, and then the money that was generated and accumulated, which made Europe much more wealthy, and so more world-oriented.

The Renaissance develops at different times and with different forms in the various parts of Europe, depending on the relative strengths of the older conservative force of the Church, and the newer liberal force of Trade. Generally speaking, in most of southern Europe where Church government was strongest, the Church eventually prevailed, and the Renaissance waned. In northern Europe, trading interests prevailed, and the Renaissance flourished.

The Renaissance took place in Florence between about 1400 and 1550. But its main roots go back to the time of Dante, Petrarch, Boccaccio and Giotto, at the beginning of the 1300's. Its effects continue at least until the end of the 1600's, by which time Florence had lost those liberties in which the Renaissance had been born.

In much of northern Europe the Renaissance begins later than in Italy, and lasts later, too. Some people argue that the political thought of the American and French Revolutions, at the end of the 18th century, had its roots in political ideas of the 15th and early 16th centuries, that the Renaissance was in effect, the whole period from the end of the Middle Ages until the beginning of modern times.

In any case, by the late 18th and early 19th century, Roman Catholic government had everywhere been reduced to a meagre part of its former power, while Roman Catholic Church law had been more or less completely displaced by commercial and scientific laws, and by those political ones which affirm the natural rights of human beings.

The same logic might argue that the Renaissance didn't really end until the Pope was arrested and imprisoned at the time of Napoleon, in 1809 – by which time Europe had finally completely discarded Papal power.

4. The Renaissance and Florence

Why was Florence so primary in this rejection of mediaeval life and of central Church government, in the search for new beliefs?

Unlike the larger towns and cities in Europe, particularly Venice and Paris, Florence at the beginning of the 15th century was essentially a new city. Most of its great buildings, its walls and its institutions were less than 100 years old – very new for the age. So it had less mediaeval legacy to discard than other cities. Its citizens were, quite simply, more modern, more forward-looking. Besides, the Florentines were naturally adept at making their own laws. Part of this would have come as inheritance from ancient Rome, and even earlier, from the Etruscans. Tuscany is, after all, named for these wonderfully civilized people who contributed so much to Rome's early development.

But more immediately, by the 13th and 14th centuries, the Florentines had become great traders. They had developed a whole practical system of procedures for trading efficiently over the whole of Europe and the Mediterranean. It was not difficult for them to develop these commercial laws into more general civil codes for everyday life.

Another reason for the earlier changes in Florence and in Italy, brought by the Renaissance, was the survival of many vestiges of the Ancient World. Throughout much of the former Roman Empire, remains of that earlier age had mostly disappeared, particularly in Europe. But not in Italy, where buildings, sculptures, *objets*, and eventually even paintings, still abounded, to be studied and incorporated more and more into modern life. Also the Italians, as the major traders in the Mediterranean, were able to discover and to buy Ancient texts which had survived, in Constantinople, or from the Arabs.

Besides, too, the Florentines had always been critical of poor Church government and had always supported Church reform. Already in the 11th century, Giovanni Gualberto preached reform on the streets of Florence, before settling in the hilly forest east of Florence, at Vallombrosa, to form an order of monks – the Servites – devoted to fighting simony, or the selling of Church favors. The greater churches in Florence – with the exception of the Cathedral – were almost all reform churches. These were to a large extent not only self-governing. They were also complex social institutions, extremely important in local Florentine life, and self-supporting financially. They were relatively independent of the Papacy in most everyday matters.

During a savage war Florence fought against the Papacy in 1375-78, as well as during the subsequent Great Schism, these reform churches became a *de facto* alternative Church government, to that of the discredited and disintegrating Papacy.

Although one can't really speak of "protestantism" before the 16th century, a sort of early Reformation, a 'protest', grew up in Florence in the latter half of the 14th, and at the beginning of the 15th centuries, in which Christians continued to worship Christ but without having any longer to believe so absolutely in the Papacy. A hundred years before Luther's reform, these churches had already become a decentralized movement, freeing Florentines from exclusive obedience to Roman Papal authority. It was from this loam of reform that humanism and the Renaissance – essentially itself a reform in which the secular came to dominate the religious – grew.

5. *The Renaissance and Today*

The Renaissance world wasn't very different from our own. It was a world of enormous change and adjustment.

For the last 200 years our world has experienced all sorts of changes, which we call revolutions: social, industrial, technological, scientific, communicative. These have not only been increasingly destructive of the predominantly static, agricultural, and nationalistic ways that people used to live, but have also been enormously liberating for humankind.

Like the Renaissance, ours is also a world where changes in the way we think bring about changes in the things we need and make. An age of re-making forms is a re-form-ing age.

Darwin, Marx, Freud, Einstein, Alexander Graham Bell, the photograph, Cézanne, Picasso, Matisse, Jackson Pollock, Proust, the Wright brothers, Henry Ford, Alexander Fleming, Gandhi, Martin Luther King – in the last hundred years or so we have developed new forms for everything. That also happened in the Renaissance:

Masaccio, Donatello, Brunelleschi, Piero della Francesca, Gutenberg, Columbus, Leonardo, Michelangelo, Machiavelli, Pontormo, Copernicus, Galileo – the list is endless.

In the Renaissance the Church was the older conservative force. Commerce, and its handmaiden, scientific advance, were the new liberating ones. Today Technology – most of which developed as a part of commerce – has become the conservative force, wanting little limit to its ever-expanding power. Ecology is the new reality. The ecological restrictions of the earth's resources limit the older Technology, grown used to endless advances. Like the Church and commerce in the Renaissance – God and Money – today the tensions between two competing forces also shape the way we live. These might be summed up similarly as – Money and Nature.

6. Florence: The World Museum of the Renaissance

In spite of all the losses from its treasures to the museums and private collections of the world, or through the destructions of time, nature and human beings, Florence still constitutes the world's only Museum of the Renaissance. In Florence are still the finest testimonials anywhere of our first steps into the modern world of artistic and scientific curiosity about the planet and about ourselves.

In the way we view the world today, we are all directly descended from the great Florentines of the Renaissance. It was they who first placed us all at the center of knowledge, and then wished as human-beings themselves, to know everything.

So Florence is literally everyone's city, where each one of us can still find our roots.

GOD AND MONEY

FLORENCE AND THE MEDICI
IN THE RENAISSANCE

God and Money

The two forces which combined to bring forth the Renaissance in Florence were the Church and Trade. The older religious one was conservative and protective of its ancient form. The new commercial force was outwardly materialistic, but really dependent upon the free spirits and the aspirations of individuals, looking to the future. Throughout the later Middle Ages, the Church and Trade both adapted, each becoming part of the other, until suddenly a third thing appeared which was neither, and at the same time both – the Renaissance.

The Medici

Significant in the development of Florentine trade, as well as in the development of the Church's temporal power in Italy, were the Medici. This family's prominence began in the early 15th century in trading and banking. Within two or three generations it had become one of the most powerful political families in Europe, the equal of kings and emperors, and stayed that way for almost three hundred years.

Early Florence and the Etruscans

For well over 2000 years before the Renaissance began in about 1400 A.D., there had been a town or city where Florence now lies. The rich Arno valley is a crossroads used from time immemorial, with passages to the north through the high Apennines, to the east and west along the Arno valley, and to the south, among the more gentle hills of Tuscany. Moreover, just where the Ponte Vecchio stands, the river narrows, and there are high banks on both sides suitable for a strong bridge.

The first Florence of which there are traces existed before the year 1000 B.C. It seems to have been inhabited by native Italic people, whoever they were. By about 700-500 B.C. Florence would have been a small village below the bigger Etruscan hill-town of Fiesole.

The Etruscans were the marvellously talented people contemporary with the ancient Greeks, who gave their name to Tuscany, and from whom modern Tuscans ultimately descend. They seem to have come to Italy from the East, even perhaps originally from Persia, or from India.

The Etruscans had many skills, all of which were absorbed into the enormous Mediterranean Empire which another Italian people, the Romans, developed across most of Europe, North Africa and the Near East. These people lived on the banks of the Tiber River at the southern edge of Tuscany, and certainly Rome was an Etruscan town before it became dominated by the Latins or Romans, as they then began to call themselves.

In architecture and engineering the Etruscans seem to have been the first to use the round arch and the barrel vault. They built the first cities in Italy. In art they loved portraits and colours, and were great jewellery makers and casters of iron and bronze. They also buried their dead in large tombs, shaped like underground houses, and often decorated these with lovely paintings. The Etruscans were wonderful farmers, who drained the valleys, and then planted the ancestors of the vines and olive trees which still florish everywhere in Tuscany. In commerce their fleets traded across much of the Western Mediterranean, through the Straits of Gibraltar into the Atlantic, and then along the west coast of Africa, or north to modern France and Great Britain. These were all things which became very important to the Romans.

In political organization the Etruscans had a league of peaceful cities, linked by strong straight roads, which seems to have been unique in the Ancient world. It became a model for the Roman Empire. In the social graces Etruscan women feasted and danced, apparently equal to men, while Etruscan patrician families became the patricians in early Roman society. In religion their sooth-sayers were famous. They were also infamously accurate, predicting even their own society's demise.

All these great civilizing elements – farming, engineering, commerce, the arts, politics, social organization and religion – became essential parts of the Roman world. Centuries later, long after the city of Rome had established its culture in all the lands surrounding the Mediterranean, and far beyond, and had then slowly decayed and collapsed, the natural talents of the Etruscans – so central to the Roman way of life and its empire – lived on, lying dormant in the Tuscan countryside.

They flowered again in the later Middle Ages and especially in the Renaissance.

ROMAN FLORENCE

Roman Florentia replaced the Etruscan Florence during the second and first century B.C. Traditionally, Florence was founded by Julius Caesar in 44 B.C., but of course that date will only indicate the Roman re-orgaization of a much earlier town. It lasted about 600 years, falling into decay during the 5th and 6th centuries after Christ, along with the general collapse of Roman civilization. The center of Roman Florence –

a grid – can still be traced on the modern map of the city, and its size can be judged by the amphitheatre which is still outlined along streets near the church of Santa Croce: in via Torta, via Bentaccordi, Piazza Peruzzi, Piazza S. Croce.

After 313 A.D. Christianity slowly became the State religion of the Roman Empire. Florence was permitted to build Christian churches. The foundation of San Lorenzo – the Medici family church – dates from this early period, as does that of the Baptistry, almost certainly built on the site of a circular Roman temple, and of Santa Reparata – the church which lies under the present Cathedral.

From about 375 A.D. onwards, as the Roman Empire weakened and then disintegrated, Italy suffered some 600 years of invasion: the Visigoths, the Vandals, the Huns, the Ostrogoths, the Longobards, the Byzantines, the Arabs, the Franks, the Magyars, the Normans. Florence became again a village, fearful for its existence. But many of these conquerors, like so many foreigners since, settled in Italy and slowly became civilized and Christianized, mixing their own energy and culture with that of Italy. To this day you will often see in Italy such family names as Tedeschi or Todeschini (Germans), Scotti (Scots), Franceschi (French), Moro or Mori (Moors), Ungaro (Hungarian), or Spagnuoli (Spaniards).

Post-Roman Florence

Europe reawakened with the Crusades. These were wars which began about the year 1100 A.D., and lasted until the middle of the 1200's. They were attempts by Christian Europe to re-conquer the Holy Land – that is, the eastern coast of the Mediterranean, where Christ had lived and died – a land which had earlier been a province of the Roman Empire. Because of these wars trade expanded considerably, as Europeans gained control of the Eastern Mediterranean and parts of the Near East. All the ports of Italy profited enormously, in particular the main ones at Venice, Genoa and Pisa. Florence also profited indirectly, especially after the years around 1200.

Christianity had been centered for centuries in rural and agricultural communities. It was static and death-oriented, and found difficulties in adjusting its doctrines of universal brotherhood and peace to the thinly veiled, expansionist intentions of the Crusades.

This was the beginning of an unholy alliance between commercialism and religion. Although it was to take many more centuries, slowly but surely the Christian religion was to become an appendage of European commercial expansion.

The growth of trade was greatly aided by Christian pilgrims, earlier tourists who wandered across Europe visiting the then historic sites--meaning those places most especially associated with Christianity and its holy relics. These travellers carried many forms of money, spending them in considerable amounts, and so stimulating the need for both modern banking, and modern money transfer and exchange. The pilgrims' freedom, too, from the old soil-based economy of the medieval feudal system was another strong sign that Europe was changing, and that individuals were becoming important. The main pilgrims' routes went south from Northern Europe to Rome, and from there on by both land and sea, to Jerusalem. But there was another important route across the Pyrenees to Spain, and to St. John of Compostella. Travellers to this last ancient pre-Christian site, where Europe ends and the great Atlantic begins, wore scallop shells, symbols of St. John. Scallop shells are still worn by pilgrims to this day.

REFORM IN THE NEW CITIES: SAINTS FRANCIS AND DOMINIC IN THE EARLY 13TH CENTURY

Many early efforts were made by the Church and by Christians to adapt Christianity to the changing world – to *re-*

form the Church. Most of these were centered in the country and amongst the clergy, and involved a stricter Christianity, a further retreat from the world. The beautiful church of San Miniato in Florence is an enduring symbol of these early monastic reforms. It was begun in the 11th century, by the Cluniacs. This order of monks was a reform of the ancient order of Benedictines, founded by a Roman, St. Benedict in the early 6th century A.D., at the time of the collapse of Rome.

But with the advent of two extraordinary reformers – Saint Francis (1182-1226) and Saint Dominic (1170-1221) – in the early years of the 13th century, the Church found revolutionaries who involved the new urban masses in a significant contemporary Christianity. These mendicants – really early socialists – wished to own nothing, living at first in the streets of the rapidly expanding cities, begging. They became so popular as well as so numerous, that within a few decades of Francis' and Dominic's deaths in the 1200's their vast numbers of followers began building monasteries and convents everywhere. These institutions became enormously rich through legacies, fulfilling in a wry way Christ's prediction that the last would be first: Santa Croce and Santa Maria Novella, respectively the Franciscan and the Dominican establisments in Florence, became also the two largest and richest architectural complexes in the city. The other large churches of SS. Annunziata, S. Maria del Carmine, Santo Spirito, Sant'Agostino, and San Marco were also reform establishments.

FLORENCE'S COMMERCE: WOOL

Florence's trade was based upon wool. Merchants would buy wool all over Europe and ship it to Florence. They would also buy dyes in the East, and alum with which to fix the colours in the cloth. Then, as today, Florentines were remarkable craftsmen, particularly good at design. Wool was worked into the most elegant sought-after cloths in Europe, and then shipped all over the known world, to be sold at handsome profit.

In order to deal with this vast trade the Florentines further developed modern concepts of money-handling: they used partnerships, limited companies, cheques, money-orders, letters-of-credit, bills of exchange, insurance policies, and, eventually, double-entry book-keeping.

It was also at this time, but not by a Florentine, that the first paper factory was opened in Christian Europe. This happened at Fabriano, south-east of Florence, in the area now called Le Marche.

Paper had been invented by a Chinese, Ts'ai Lun, in about 105 A.D. Knowledge of the process reached the Arab world in the 8th century, but they managed to keep the process secret from Christian Europe until the mid-twelve-hundreds. This was probably because European trading techniques were so simple and Europeans so uneducated until then, that there was little need of paper. Without inexpensive paper the development of long-distance trade, and thus of modern capitalism, would have been difficult, if not impossible. Scientific inquiry, also, could hardly have developed without paper.

This invention of paper-making, together with the invention in about 1450, and development of moveable type for printing, are two events which percipitate the change in European life from the static Christian Middle Ages, to a society which was more fluid and inter-dependant, more nature oriented, scientific and democratic. The development of printing in particular, so similar to the more recent development of computers, also took but a few decades to revolutionize life.

It was from the vast profits of an ever richer commercial community that the Renaissance then grew. Florence was at the center of all this change, and its profits were lent out all over Europe at huge interest rates. So much money was accumulated in Florence in this way that the Florentines coined their own money, based upon a gold florin. This became the great international currency, the dollar of its day.

Use of this early gold-standard facilitated the still further development of modern trading centers – cities – and of modern capitalism, while causing the inevitable withering of medieval rural economy.

But money-lending for interest, called usury, was actually forbidden by the static Church, which understood the dangers for its own existance which the power and fluidity of money represented. So conflict developed between the Church, dominated in the cities by the reformed orders of Franciscans and Dominicans claiming poverty, and the increasingly wealthy business community. And as the new traders became independant, the Church became in turn, jealous and afraid of them.

In that conflict the *Age of Faith* died. However in its resolution the Renaissance, and the modern world, were born.

USURY AND ART

Although it was sinful for businessmen to charge high interest rates, the Church let it be known that adequate and beautiful gifts, offered to God through his Church might assuage men's guilt. The size and quality of the gift might possibly be relevant to the amount of eventual forgiveness after death...

Because of this, the adorning of churches increased in direct proportion to the wealth generated by the trading community, as did the quality of the offerings involved. These were allowed to become larger and more ornate, and of course thus more world-oriented.

By the ploy of condemning interest the Church absorbed into itself much of the wealth of the business world, changing forever the form of that wealth from money into art. Over a period of several hundred years artists produced literally millions of exquisitely crafted objects, while Christianity continued, with this arrangement to exert its influence upon and through businessmen. Not surprisingly, it was by way of this Church-directed arrangement that art began to replace God as Western society's object of veneration.

This happened because it is always the artist who, regardless of language or location or Age, constantly indicates truth. Art is universal to us all. Whether music or painting or architecture, sculpture, pottery, jewellery, dance, photography – whatever – it's our common language. The more artistic a creation, the more universal it is. In the Renaissance the artist was employed by both the Church and by the businessman, to impart spirituality where otherwise it wouldn't have existed. The collaboration of the two produced some of the finest creations ever made.

For all of society the artist slowly became the accepted magician, a high priest, more important than popes or kings, more important than the richest trader, able to justify and transform the growing materialism of man. Only the artist was able to turn materialistic profit into art, uniting both vital parts of man's character, the materialistic and the spiritual. In fact the grand Renaissance artist became the new priest of society.

This, of course, suited the businessman perfectly. Without the spiritual input of the artist, all his money and materialism was worthless, dispersed as he himself decayed. Money in fact, represented the flesh, while the artist and art represented God. It was only the artist who, especially through the portrait

– a form of memory, could slowly help man convince himself that he, and not Christ, was God.

Much later, when Christianity had lost its enormous influence on European life, the artist who expresses the spiritual side of man's nature, the side of ideas, of emotions, of instinct, of vision, of love – found he had less and less place in an increasingly materialistic society. Many static, middleclass traders, whose primary belief was in the accumulation of wealth and in possessions, no longer believers in God, found they had no need of spiritual values or of the artist who disturbed their life by expressing them. Others, who could see the abyss to which materialism leads, recognized the artist as the last spiritual hope of the West.

The ultimate, nearly total displacement of Western spiritual values by materialistic ones took place during the late 18th, and 19th centuries. It signalled the final end of even the last echoes of the Renaissance, born as the Renaissance had been of both spiritual and materialistic parents. At that point there was little, or no place at all, within society for the true artist, the whole person, who is both spiritual and worldly.

So eventually the artist became *The Outsider* – to use the English title for Camus' masterpiece, *L'Étranger*. Cézanne, Van Gogh, Gauguin, Modigliani, Soutine – the end of the last century and much of the present one, are full of examples of great men who could only make their statements on the margins of materialistic society. And of course today in our world of near total materialism, the artistic creations of an earlier age are of enormous value to us, while our money is of little – as can so easily be seen by the prices now paid for art at auction.

A New city: The 13th and 14th centuries

By 1260 the Bargello, the new Town Hall, had been built, to be followed fifty years later by an even larger one – Palazzo della Signoria, now called Palazzo Vecchio. This still houses many of the city's municipal offices.

There were three bridges over the Arno, in addition to the single one that had been there since Roman times. Between 1260 and 1340 Santa Croce, Santa Maria Novella, Or San Michele, the Cathedral, the Palazzo Vecchio, and Ponte Vecchio were all started, and in great part finished. New city walls were constructed enclosing such extensive land that much of it wasn't built over until the 19th century. Santa Trinita, the Badia, Santa Maria Maggiore, San Remigio, San Giovanni Cavalieri, and Santo Stefano al Ponte were all rebuilt.

In painting Giotto (c.1267-1337) appeared, to invent a picture of ordinary man who seemed for the first time in Christian art to be alive and important. In these years too, Dante (1255-1321) did much the same thing in literature, when he wrote the *Divine Comedy*, summing up the beliefs of the mediaeval world in modern form. Together with Petrarch (1304-1374) and Boccaccio (1313-1375), Dante established Florentine as a language equal to the Latin which all educated men had used since the downfall of Rome. It is of course Florentine which has become the everyday language of today's Italy.

THE APPEARANCE OF THE MEDICI

Many new trading families appeared in this period at the end of the 1200's and the first decades of the 1300's, to displace the old landed aristocracy. For two of them, the Bardi and the Peruzzi, Giotto painted in the church of Santa Croce revolutionary images of a three-dimensional human being.

Although it was to be almost one hundred years before they began to show themselves as distinguished as had been the great banking families of the early 14th century, among those new trading families were also the Medici – a family which came to Florence from the Mugello, the large, rich mountain valley of the river Sieve, some 25 kilometers to the north of Florence, the same valley in fact where Giotto was born.

By 1340 Florence was essentially a new city, as rich and as large as Paris and Venice, the largest in Europe. Its two civic gathering points were clearly defined, marking the two major forces in the city: the older center was the area around the Baptistry of San Giovanni and the new Cathedral then being built, of Santa Maria del Fiore; the other center was in front of the big new Town Hall, Palazzo della Signoria, then one of the the largest civil structures in Italy.

But Florence's role in that modern world was much more important than Paris or Venice, or any other city in Europe. Aside from the Florentine banks which dominated much of European trade and finance, and thereby much of European politics, Florence's cultural role was foremost – showing that Florentines were looking forward to a future new world where Man would order, and even try to dominate nature.

The development of humanism – the new human-oriented attitudes which reflected the development of the new city – was clearly seen in the vast program of statues, mostly made between the late 1300's and the 1420's for the exterior of the Cathedral, for its Bell Tower, and for the exterior of Or San Michele – a grain market which bad been converted into a shrine and church after the Black Death. These statues, 34 of them, all conceived quite separately from their architectural niches which had been built earlier – were begun in the late Gothic forms of the end of the Middle Ages. But as the first two decades of the 1400's developed, the forms changed, and became – particularly under the influence of Donatello – humanistic. For the Florentines of the day, who watched new statues being put up every few years, it must have been an exhilarating moment, each statue more "realistic" than the last, each statue more world-oriented. Not since Roman times had such a program of large, detached statues been undertaken in any Western society.

THE DISASTERS WHICH CLEARED THE WAY FOR THE RENAISSANCE

Between 1330 and 1420 Florence went through a series of traumatic shocks which served to destroy forever its citizens' belief in the old order of things, and to push the city towards its destiny. Just as a person who has been desperately ill rises from the sick-bed determined to change his or her life, so Florence rose from the agonies of the 14th century determined to reform its own way of life – to give it new forms.

At first Florence suffered flood (1333), bankruptcy (1342), decades of economic stagnation, and the Bubonic Plague. In the summer months of 1348 this last – known ever since as the Black Death – killed as many as 50,000 people, roughly half the city's population. Then, only a few years later, in a profound disagreement over the Papacy's territorial claims, the city waged a brutal war against the Pope. The entire Florentine population was excommunicated, that is forbidden to practice the rites of Catholicism or to receive the sacraments.

Many of Florence's priests continued nonetheless to say the mass and to distribute communion, creating a serious precedent of communal independence from the Papacy.

Apart from the Cathedral, Florence's largest churches were built by the reforming orders. Besides the Franciscans and the Dominicans, the other main reform orders were the Augustinian Friars, the Carmelites, and the Servites. Their large establishments constituted, together with other smaller reform churches, a sort of almost independent, decentralized Christian church within the main church organization run by the Pope, and centered in the unfinished Cathedral. As already noted, Santa Croce and Santa Maria Novella were the Franciscan and Dominican complexes. Those of the Augustinians, Carmelites, and Servites were S. Spirito, Sant'Agostino, S. Maria del Carmine, and Santissima Annunziata.

There was also a workers' revolution in 1378, a war against Milano in 1402 when Florence nearly lost its ancient trading liberties, and another war against Naples in 1414.

But most disruptive of all, Florence was at the center of the *Great Schism* of the Church, when there were first two popes, then three, and then for a short moment, four – two of whom lived side-by-side in Florence.

THE GREAT SCHISM: 1378-1417

The Great Schism was the final death throe of Mediaeval Christianity, the ultimate sign of the profound difficulty the Christian Church was having with survival in the modern world of trade and the freedom trade engenders.

Saints Francis and Dominic, together with their followers and other reformers, had regenerated and popularized the Church in the late 12th and 13th centuries. But they hadn't acted through Papal organization. They'd acted in spite of it, or even against it, appealing directly to the people.

Man's increasing mobility of mind and body, the increasing awareness of the natural world and love for it, were more and more incompatible with the static hierarchical ideas of mediaeval Papal teaching. The ecclesiastical authorities insisted that Christians believe not only in Christ but also in the teachings of 'His' temporal Church.

Worse: it became increasingly clear that 'Popes', as well as many of the other Church authorities, were willing to behave hypocritically, and in ways that they themselves condemned as seriously immoral.

By the end of the 14th century it was not at all clear which of a number of men claiming to be Pope represented Christ's Church... So Christians went on believing in Christ, but less in his multiple Popes, or in their temporal Church. This was the beginning of the first phase of the Reformation which terminated at the time of Luther, a hundred years later.

The Great Schism happened between 1378 and 1417. There had been such squabbles within the Church government, over a long period, that two separate Popes were elected – an Avignon Pope and a Roman one. Then a third Pope was elected at Pisa to try to eliminate the other two. This third Pope was in some ways also a Florentine Pope, as Pisa belonged then to Florence. Finally all three lines were either deposed or quit, and a fourth Pope was elected at Constance, in southern Germany. This last Pope obviously claimed – as had the other three – that he was the only legitimate one. It is in descent from this fourth line of Popes that the present Pope claims his own authority.

The Renaissance can be seen as a new re-forming of Christianity. But instead of a reform of clergy, like all the earlier reforms, it was a reform and a liberalization of the whole secular body of the church, the Christian lay population of Europe.

Or the Renaissance can be also seen as the beginning of a return by Europeans to a pre-Christian way of viewing life, a return which used the relics of the worlds of Ancient Rome, and eventually also of Ancient Greece, as guides.

During the later Renaissance, particularly in northern Europe, the discredited clergy was displaced as the most important element in Christian organization, by ordinary Christians. This was, in a real sense, the beginnings of what we call modern democracy.

THE ARRIVAL OF THE MEDICI AND THE TOMB OF POPE JOHN XXIII: 1419

A symbol of this new detachment from the Papacy, and also of the arrival of both the Medici family, and of the Renaissance, as prime actors upon the Florentine scene, is the tomb of Pope John XXIII. He was one of the various schismatic Popes in the early years of the 15th century, one of the Pisan Popes. By chosing the small, little-known Medici bank to handle papal finances, John XXIII brought the Medici into the center of modern politics, as well as substantially increasing their wealth.

Pope John XXIII died in 1419. As a gesture intended to express both their gratitude to him, as well as their attitude towards his role in attempting to give re-birth to the Church, Giovanni and Cosimo Medici – father and son heads of the family at that time – had him buried in solitary state in the temple of re-birth, the Florentine Baptistry. They also commissioned a fine sepulchre to be made by Donatello and Michelozzo. It is one of the first monuments in the new Renaissance mode, and apt that it should have been greatly paid for by the family which, for the next 300 years were destined to become the greatest Florentine Renaissance family, as well as the greatest art patrons of all European history.

Across the tomb the Medici inscribed in Latin, *John XXIII-Quandam Papa*, that is, "Sometime Pope". The then newly-elected Roman pontiff, Martin V, who was the first of the fourth line of Popes, objected to this, claiming that John XXIII had been but an anti-Pope – that is, not a true Pope. However at that point in history, commerce unquestionably still took precedence in Florence over the Roman Church. The two bankers' inscription remained. After a short period of ostracism, the Medici were also re-installed as the Papal bankers. This soon made them the richest people in Europe.

So deep was the wound of the Great Schism that over 500 years later another Roman Catholic Pope in our own day chose the name John XXIII, to emphasize yet again that for the Papacy in Rome, the earlier John XXIII had never been Pope.

Neo-Gothic nostalgia before the Renaissance

During this period of despair from the 1340's until about 1415-20, most of the world-view, the laws and beliefs which had been unquestioned truth for centuries, collapsed. Many Florentines looked backwards, hoping that the old mediaeval God would save them. Their art throughout this period is called neo-Gothic and expressed a desire to return to a pre-Giotto, mediaeval, Gothic world where God had dominated every thought, and legislated every good or evil.

But most Florentines, particularly the artistic leaders, having passed through the traumatic experiences of the Schism, and having begun to experience a slow return to economic prosperity, turned again to look forward.

They began to feel themselves freed of old mediaeval beliefs, and powerful enough to discover new natural ones. Over the next decades, Florentines abandoned many of the old civil and religious laws of the preceeding centuries, and began to search for, discover, and define significant truths about themselves and about nature, new laws to bolster and replace their disenchantment with traditional Christianity. This re-shaping of thought so that its form became an amalgam of belief in man and belief in Christ, with man emerging more dominantly than Christ, affected everything they touched.

Consequently, it was in the 1420's, just after the Schism had passed that Masaccio, Donatello, and Brunelleschi affirmed so significantly the future direction of Western thought and Western art: Masaccio was born in 1401, Donatello in 1386, and Brunelleschi in 1377.

MASACCIO (1401-1428)

Masaccio – who's name means "Big Tom" (from Tomasaccio) – painted people free-standing in space, modelled either on human beings themselves, or on ancient Roman statues. The heads in the Tribute Money, Masaccio's great masterpiece, painted in the Brancacci Chapel in the church of Santa Maria del Carmine, around 1425, seem to be drawn after Roman portrait sculptures: Caracalla, Septimus Severus, Hercules, Herodotus, and others. Besides the figures are all cloaked in Roman togas, and standing as though posed in an ancient Roman relief sculpture.

Masaccio painted a natural light falling upon his grand figures, producing dramatic *chiaroscuro* effects on their faces – that is, effects of shading made by falling light. The figures cast strong shadows. People are shown as strong-willed beings, apparently free to decide their own fate, dominant in the world of nature spread out around them. The only sign that the figures are still Christian are the halos.

The painting shows Christ telling St Peter, who represents the Church in Rome, to pay a tax to the State – another poignant indication of the relationship of the Church to trade in 1425. In fact, all the paintings by Masaccio in the Brancacci Chapel are about the role of St Peter in the Church's religious life, and so refer to the precarious political position of the Papacy in the early 15th century.

In particular the fresco of *The Raising of the Son of Theophilus* seems to be a reflection on the role the Papacy should play in Italian political life. On the left is a figure representing the Governor of Antioch, holding a staff of authority – he is the State. On the right is St Peter enthroned, but devoid of any symbol of worldly power. He is again, as in the other frescoes, the Church. In between is St Peter bringing the Governor's son back to life after the boy had been dead many years.

The Governor looks across at St Peter who is seated higher, praying, as though the picture were stating that the State takes its advice and support from the miraculous powers of the Church, rather than from the Church's temporal or worldly powers. The boy seems to represent nothing less than the resuscitation of the Italian State after many years of death. There had been no single Italian State since the collapse of the Roman Empire, many centuries before. It was precisely at the beginning of the Renaissance that Italian thinkers and writers began to hope once again for a united Italy, just as other countries in Europe, particularly England, France, and Spain, were becoming more unified and powerful. From the new city of Florence, sometimes seen as the New Jerusalem, would rise the new Italy. But the problem of the relationship between the Church and State was so intractable that one hundred years later Machiavelli was still lamenting that the only impediment to the resurrection of a united Italy was the Church. And in fact, it took until the 19th century for Italy to unify, and that only happened through its subjugation by Napoleon, who dispossessed the Church of all its temporal power.

There was a rumour in the Renaissance that Masaccio, who died at the early age of 26, had been poisoned. If it is true that he was murdered, it might well have been at the orders of some Papal official, perhaps one of the important Cardinals such as Branda Castiglione, or even the ambitious Pope Martin V himself, frightened by the power of Masaccio's bold new statements. The Pope had been elected by the Council of Constance only a few years before, and not by the Cardinals in conclave, as Church law requires. So the new Pope's attempt to restore Papal power was disputed by many.

Before the late Middle-Ages and early Renaissance most people never saw pictures, except rarely and only as religious illustrations, always in churches. Masaccio's new, starkly realistic depictions of the Church as subordinate in and to a secular world must have appeared to most ordinary Florentines as stunningly apt. But to Roman Church officials these same pictures must have seemed heretical and very dangerous. It is poignant that Masaccio's assumed self-portrait, the face in the Theophilus fresco to the right of St. Peter's throne, looks not at the first Pope, St. Peter, but directly at us...

The fresco opposite the *Raising of the Son of Theophilus*, although painted some fifty years later by Filippino Lippi, must be on an original wall-drawing, – a sinopia – by Masaccio. The picture refers to simony, or the granting of church favors in exchange for money. This was a particularly noxious and commonplace practice among Christian clerics of the day, and one of the prime causes of Church reform.

MASACCIO AND LINEAR PERSPECTIVE

Masaccio introduced systematic linear perspective into painting, so that his pictures do not seem to be on a flat wall. Instead they seem almost as though on theater-stages set into the wall, full of a new direct light which comes from a single source – an imaginary sun somewhere within the painting's world, and above it. The space the artist creates seems to extend to an imaginary horizon deep inside the make-believe space of the picture.

This deep illusionary space, shaped as though inside an imaginary cone or box tapering to an imaginary vanishing point, brought a new dimension of movement into painting, and consequently a new dimension of beauty. In earlier painting the vision depicted by painters was two-dimensional, so that the eye's function was blocked more or less at or near the surface of the picture. It could only move on the flat plane.

With Masaccio's enormous development, vision and sight seemed to move to the inside of the picture, carrying us into the imaginary space. Since that space of the picture didn't really exist, the possibilities of imaginary movement were not only endless, they were immaterial, and in this sense, spiritual. The sensation of movement became almost like an echo of music, the apparition of an idea, vibrations of color oscillating between our own real world, and that insubstantial one within the picture. This was both thoroughly abstract, as well as real, concrete in our physical presence, the eye passing from the real to an unreal world made to appear real. As such we enter a limitless spiritual world where the imagination of each one of us is the center.

More: by creating a fake real world as it might have been, Masaccio gave space to memory, essential to the Renaissance. In medieval Christian life, man had no need of memory, as people gave little heed to this material world, seen only as a stepping-stone to eternal life in heaven, after death. But when the Christian God failed, humans suddenly appeared naked and alone. They needed memory to feel sure of their own existence. It's Masaccio's kind of painting, where the fake becomes real – propaganda, if you like – which provides a new and modern image of how we have been in the past. It was money which caused the Renaissance, but it was a need for memory which sustained it: the need to know who we are, and thus from whence we come. Making pictures in the Renaissance grew into the grandest of all the arts, as it still is

– but now often with film – from this need of humans to alleviate the new terror of perhaps not existing.

Masaccio developed a whole new concept of Man, picturing him no longer minute and passing, but dominant in the world of Nature. Christ had dominated the mediaeval world. Masaccio transformed ordinary man into a new, secular Christ, to dominate the new, modern world. Paradoxically, just as scientists and explorers began to take apart the natural world, Masaccio, at the beginning of the 15th century, showed how it is possible, using only the emotions, to build up a whole new spiritual but secular world, by means of art. This was a great discovery, that the world of emotion inside each individual person was real, and limitless. It was a discovery which harked back to the writings of a late Roman: St Augustine.

Tradition has often attributed to Filippo Brunelleschi, the architect, the invention of linear perspective. Certainly he may have invented it. But a need to imitate the space of the natural world appears at the same time in both Florentine and north European painting, a need to project man's movement in a spacious, trading world.

Conversely, architects had built the hundreds of Gothic abbeys and cathedrals of the mediaeval world without apparent knowledge of linear perspective. So for what purpose did the architect Brunelleschi invent it?

It seems more probable that a painter of Masaccio's enormous creative imagination and skill developed it through studying earlier painting, and reading the optical studies of the Arab writer Al-Hazen which had then become available. Also, Masaccio would have studied shadows: shadows from candle-flames in any of the night-time rooms of Masaccio's pre-electricity world formed, as do shadows from the sun itself, a single-point linear perspective arrangement to the flame's light.

All through the 14th century painters tried to imitate or to portray natural space in a logical convincing way. By the first quarter of the 15th century, some of them – particularly the Flemish in the north, and to a lesser extent, some painters from the Marches area of Italy to the south-east of Florence, and some from Siena, had become adept at it. Masaccio himself, in his earliest picture we know, dated 1422, when he was only 20, shows that he already understood the basic rules of one-point linear perspective. Masaccio may actually have been trained by Giovanni Toscani, one of the few Florentine painters of the early 1400's who showed an interest in perspective and chiaroscuro.

From a candle's light it is also easy to study the effects of chiaroscuro, as well as the way cast light parallels the apparent cone-like function of the eye as we 'cast our glance', like a beam of light, on the world about us.

This image of man standing free, dominating nature while still an integral part of it, was to remain the principal subject matter of European painting until the time of the French painter Cézanne, in the late 1800's, when much painting had already become displaced by the photograph.

Until that time Western man continued to believe he was uniquely superior in nature, and could eventually know nature completely, and control it all.

PAINTING THEN AND NOW

Not surprisingly the artistic forms of painting which grew up during the roughly fifty years after Masaccio's death in 1428, are not unsimilar in their variety to those which followed Cézanne's death in 1906.

Masaccio created a replica of our own natural world, put the sun's light into it, and expanded the space within it to the horizon. He then placed inside this new image, a human being who moved, and who dominated.

After Masaccio's death artists investigated many aspects of his new imaginary world: light, linear and atmospheric perspective, apparent space, surface values, physiognomy and anatomy, colour, every element and every object of the natural world, the significance of action, – but above all else, human beings.

Four hundred and fifty years later, due in part to the invention of photography, which was a late popular development of Masaccio's way of seeing the world – Cézanne didn't actually take man out of painting, but he took away man's dominant role. Cézanne returned man to what he is: an integral part of developing nature, just like everything else, intertwined, growing with nature, and dependent upon it.

Cézanne made the painting more important than Man, or anyway as important as Man. And most of the painters who followed Cézanne investigated abstract aspects of a painting's structure: colour, shape, texture, design, mark, medium, or whatever, instead of using the painting to investigate or describe human beings and the natural world around them. Of course abstraction is elementary to the natural world, so, in that sense, Masaccio's great influence continues today.

Probably Masaccio was the most influential painter who ever lived, and his two pictures, *The Trinity*, and *The Tribute Money*, the two most influential pictures ever painted. His only obvious rival would be Giotto: but Giotto ended the Middle Ages, whereas Masaccio began the modern world.

From the early Renaissance onwards, the narrative in European painting becomes "realistic", and splits into three main themes: landscape, portrait, and still-life. The common interest remains always a wish to know everything about human beings, and nature.

In the 19th century, and the opening years of this one, Darwin, Marx, Freud, Einstein and a host of other liberated thinkers many of them Jewish, and thus free of Christian prejudice, threw off the ancient Euro-Christian blinkers, to reveal how integral a part of a great macrocosm we really are. They understood that it is always nature which governs Man, and not the contrary, and nature which will destroy us if we do not attune ourselves within its basic realities.

DONATELLO (c. 1386-1466)

As Masaccio humanized painting, Donatello humanized sculpture. His statues start as religious decoration for buildings. But soon they step down, so to speak, into the streets and piazzas of Florence, to appear as real people, hardly religious at all. And if they are religious, it is already a re-formed Christianity, no longer that of a mediaeval Papal hierarchy, but one modelled on ordinary men and women in the Florentine streets. Belief in Christ becomes an interior, personal credo, rather than an exterior, Church-directed one.

No single object more poignantly expresses this new fusion of God-in-Man than Donatello's *Christ-Figure-on-a-Cross*, made for Cosimo Medici at Bosco ai Frati in the Mugello, north of Florence.

BRUNELLESCHI (1377-1446)

Filippo Brunelleschi was the architect who built the dome on Florence's Cathedral, the largest dome created between Roman times and the Renaissance. Brunelleschi built it without scaffolding, constructing it upon itself, a symbol of the whole Renaissance, Man's grasp and use of natural law realized upon a heroic scale. The cupola of the Cathedral is by itself a perfect octagonal Renaissance structure, placed on top of an earlier 14th century building.

Brunelleschi was the architect, too, of the churches of San Lorenzo and Santo Spirito, of the Ospedale degli Innocenti, and of the Cappella Pazzi, humanizing architecture so that it reflects primarily Man's intellect, the needs of our mind. Compared to earlier Romanesque and Gothic buildings, the interiors of these structures seem almost Protestant in their cold, elegant logic. And indeed, many years before Luther, they are already products of that re-forming of thought which made the Renaissance.

Cosimo Medici (1389-1464) and the Renaissance

The two bankers Giovanni and Cosimo Medici, father and son, who had commmissioned the tomb for the body of John XXIII, were the first members of the family to have more than local importance. Giovanni was born in 1360 and Cosimo died in 1464. In the one hundred years that their two lives spanned, they lifted their family from the level of an ordinary Florentine commercial one, to among the richest and most influential in all European history.

Both were important patrons, but it was Cosimo who set a standard of taste and patronage which has perhaps never been equalled in the life of a single man. Certainly no person since the ancient world had been such a patron. After Cosimo had been dead some years a small secret book was found, in which Medici contributions between 1434 and 1471 to artistic works, to charities and to taxes had been carefully noted: something in the order of 200-300 million dollars had been spent in today's terms. And the list only begins when Cosimo was nearly 45 years old...

There was hardly a major Florentine artist of his time who was not patronized by Cosimo. If it could be said that any single human being provided the enlightened energy which caused the Renaissance to blossom in Florence, that catalyst would have to be Cosimo Medici. He was the essential link between two almost antagonistic philosophies, the Church and Trade, *God and Money.*

It was during Cosimo's long lifetime – he was born in 1389, in the late Middle Ages, and died at 75, in the full-flower of the Renaissance – that the cupola of the Cathedral was built, that Masaccio painted his revolutionary frescoes in S. Maria Novella and S. Maria del Carmine, and that Donatello, Nanno di Banco (1380/90-1421), and Luca della Robbia (1399-1482), re-formed sculpture in the image of man. Donatello was three years older than Cosimo and outlived him by two years. As Cosimo neared death Donatello was still working for him, completing the *Judith and Holofernes* for the garden of Palazzo Medici, in about 1460. In fact, Donatello went on working for Cosimo even after the latter's death – on the bronze pulpits now in San Lorenzo. Businessman and artist had collaborated for almost 50 years.

Cosimo and the Golden age of the Renaissance: 1420-1464

Lorenzo Monaco (1370?-1423), Fra Angelico (1387/1400-1455), Masolino (1387?-?1440), Filippo Lippi (1406-1462), Domenico Veneziano (1400-1461), Paolo Uccello (1397-1475), Benozzo Gozzoli (1420-1497), Andrea del Castagno (1423-1457), Baldovinetti (1425-1499), Verocchio (1435-1488) – also all worked during Cosimo's lifetime, as did many other artists. There is no common style to their work because each man sought out his own vision of reality without any pressure from the weakened Church, or from Cosimo's liberal, enlightened State.

Lorenzo Ghiberti (1378-1455) also worked during Cosimo's time, when he made both his magnificent pairs of doors for the Baptistry. Andrea della Robbia(1435-1525), Bernardo

(1409-1464) and Antonio (1427-1479) Rosellino, Desiderio da Settignano (1428-1464), and Mino da Fiesole (1430-1484), all also live and sculpted in Florence during Cosimo's lifetime.

During the first half of the 15th century, in addition to constructing the Cathedral dome, Brunelleschi rebuilt San Lorenzo for Cosimo, including the Old Sacristy, and designed Santo Spirito. He also designed and built most of the Ospedale degli Innocenti in Piazza SS. Annunziata, and designed the nearby S. Maria degli Angeli.

Leon Battista Alberti (1406-1472), a Florentine exile and great theoretician of architecture, returned to Florence in the 1430's to design the front of Palazzo Ruccellai, the beautiful loggia opposite, as well as the classical Sepulchre in the family's private chapel behind the palazzo. He also completed the design for the facade of Santa Maria Novella.

Besides the palazzo which Michelozzo Michelozzi (1396-1472) built as a town residence for Cosimo in the middle of Florence, now called Palazzo Riccardi, Michelozzo also enlarged and built him villas in the country, at Careggi (1457) and Fiesole (1458-61), and in the Mugello at Trebbio (1461) and Cafaggiolo (1451), where the Medici had owned land for generations. Nearby to these last homes of the Medici, Michelozzo built the little church at Bosco ai Frati, for Cosimo to stay in and pray in, during his old age.

Michelozzo rebuilt much of the church of San Marco for Cosimo, in particular the beautiful library (1444). For Cosimo was also the greatest bibliophile of his day, buying books all over the world, particularly texts from the Ancient world, and bringing them to Florence to be studied and translated.

Cosimo was above all an astute politician and a great statesman. Although one of the richest men in the world, and among the most famous, throughout his long life he never claimed for himself more rights than those of an ordinary citizen. After he died in 1464 the town decided that this extraordinary man should forever be known as Pater Patriae, the Father of Florence. Perhaps he was that, the greatest Florentine ever, whose business and political sense made the work of so many others possible.

Not since the heroic days of ancient Greece and Periclean Athens had any community in the West been so liberated from its past, so charged and so transformed by free, original thought, as Florence in the time of Cosimo Medici.

LORENZO IL MAGNIFICO: 1449-1492. THE CALM BEFORE THE STORM

Cosimo's only surviving son, Piero, who was born in 1416, inherited the government of Florence for only five years from 1464 to 1469. Piero was called 'the Gouty'. He suffered all his life from ill health, and his short time as Florence's untitled ruler was without important changes.

But his son, Cosimo's grandson, Lorenzo, who came to be called Il Magnifico (1449-1492), was as intelligent and as politically adroit as the grandfather. Like Cosimo, he ruled Florence as its first citizen, taking care to maintain the city's outwardly republican appearance. Unlike his grandfather, Lorenzo had a short life. He came to power in 1469 aged 20 and died aged 44. Throughout his rule the Renaissance continued to flower. But by the time be died in 1492, the delicate balance between ecclesiastical and commercial power which Cosimo and he had hoped to maintain, collapsed.

Unfortunately, Cosimo's role as Papal banker, together with the Medici policy of exiling competitors, tied Florence more and more to a single source of income, and not an industrial source: the Pope. Since the Papacy was one of the main political and geographic powers in Italy, this meant that Florence's political policies became less and less its own. Florence slowly but irretrievably lost its original source of energy – competetive manufacture, merchandising, and banking – to become mere agent for a single more powerful patron.

Besides, by the end of the 15th century, Italian trade had become secondary in a Europe more and more dominated by the Nation-States: the Netherlands, Spain, Portugal, France, and England. Meanwhile, Papal power which had been almost eclipsed a century before at the time of the Great Schism, permitting Florentine liberties to flourish, became by the end of the 15th century, firmly re-established in Rome. It also became ruthless.

Great men – Lorenzo il Magnifico's younger contemporaries – went on to make some of the most interesting works of the Renaissance: Machiavelli (1469-1527), Leonardo (1452-1519), Michelangelo (1475-1564). But more and more they made them in exile, or away from Florence: Machiavelli at his farm outside the city, Leonardo in Milano and in France, Michelangelo in Rome. There was less and less business money in Florence and consequently less power, and less freedom.

The world of trade demanded liberty to move about the physical world, and freedom to take the necessary decisions for the betterment of trade. That of Christianity obligated all primary movement to be away from the same physical world, towards a spiritual ideal. Sadly, as the 15th century unfolded, the Christian Church center at Rome, demanded more and more that the primary movement of its subjects – as they became – be not even spiritual towards God, but only towards the Church's worldly government itself.

Great tension developed all over Italy as the second half of the 15th century drew towards its conclusion. A series of fairly worldly popes, apparently almost oblivious to the spiritual condition of Christianity, involved the Church in political alliances which gave the Church temporal power but lost it spiritually. The paintings of Sandro Botticelli (1445-1510) – in particular the two now in the Uffizi, the *Birth of Venus* and *The Return of Spring* – express an attempt among Florentine thinkers to reconcile the philosophy of the ancient Greeks with 15th century Roman Catholic doctrine. Both paintings are images of Venus, who represents ideal love here on earth. She also symbolizes divine grace, through which Christians believe they can attain heaven.

After Lorenzo Medici died it was clear that Florence's position as a major economic force in Europe was already over. In that year of 1492, Christian Spain, after 800 years of war and occupation, managed finally to break the last remaining Arab power in Europe.

And of course, that was the year Columbus – an Italian from Genova – discovered and claimed the "New World" for Spain, suddenly making that country the richest and most powerful in Europe. America was named for another Italian, a Florentine, the cartographer Amerigo Vespucci, who had been an employee of the Medici bank, a protégé of Lorenzo's, and had lived with him at his hunting castle, Trebbio. Without major money in Florence, there was no longer the productive tension between Trade and Church which had fired such energy for so long. Symptomatic of this was the closure of the Medici bank after Lorenzo's death.

SAVONAROLA (1452-1498)

Even during Lorenzo's lifetime, the upset of that finely tuned equilibrium produced Girolamo Savonarola, a religious fanatic, precursor of Luther's more moderate and more successful Reformation. This Dominican priest was from Ferrara. He became attached to the monastery at San Marco. Savonarola taught that the solution to Florence's problems was to turn the clock back and make the city into a Republic of Christ, with himself at its head. Unchecked by any major commercial or trading establishment within the city, he was able for a number of years to preach bigoted, increasingly anti-humanistic messages of doom. Finally in 1498 the Papacy, fearful that he was usurping its own role, had him burned at the stake in Piazza Signoria.

DECLINE OF THE FLORENTINE RENAISSANCE: 1492-1530

John XXIII's elegant tomb with its defiant inscription 'Some-Time Pope' had signalled, at the beginning of the century, the ascendancy of Florentine trade over the Church. The plaque in Piazza della Signoria marking the spot of Savonarola's execution by the Papacy, signals the Roman Church's ascendancy at the end.

In the last analysis it was the domination of Trade over Church which produced the Renaissance in Florence. The opposite domination, of Church over Trade, began at the beginning of the 16th century to alter the substance of the Renaissance. Then, slowly, as the century progressed in Florence, this ascendency destroyed that original substance of freedom entirely.

Florence lived in a sort of limbo during the years between the death of Lorenzo il Magnifico in 1492, and the town's conquest by a Spanish army in 1530.

Every one of the major thinkers in Florence expresses the high tension of this period of danger. People could not see forward, of course. But the sensitive ones, even if unconsciously, realized that the serious imbalance between commercial activity and the Church was enormously dangerous for a city whose whole development was based upon the wealth and freedom of its trading community.

Between 1492 and 1530 the Church dominated Florentine life, in great part through two Medici popes, in a way it had not done since the days following the Black Death, 150 years previously. This awareness of great danger is clear in Machiavelli's writings. It's evident in Leonardo da Vinci's enigmatic life and work. And it's supremely evident in the lack of serenity and completion in much of Michelangelo's sculpture: the tomb for Pope Julius II, which Michelangelo worked on much of his life, is a prime example. The project was conceived to exalt a man who claimed to be the descendent and heir of St. Peter – God's holy representative on earth. But the man, and the monument, had so little to do with the aims and aspirations of Christ or of his disciples that it was probably the antithesis of them. Not surprisingly, Michelangelo was never able to complete the tomb.

How, after all, could even that great artist sculpt or paint a perfect Christian in an age when Christ's Church was so far from perfection? Or, even more fundamentally: how could he portray a Christian as perfect, when Christians by definition are, from birth until death, irrevocably marred by original sin?

The great tragedy in Michelangelo's life is that he lived and worked in such a pseudo-religious age. His patrons wished him to express truth in its visual form, beauty, when they themselves were so untruthful. They wanted Michelangelo to express a static, falsely heirarchical world when reality all about them was in movement and developing naturally.

Artists turn more and more to themes from the Old Testament and from Greek mythology, where the figures are pre-Christian, in order to avoid this difficult reality in their attempt to be both good Christians, good artists, and – even more difficult – good Christian artists.

Michelangelo's *David*, an extraordinary statue on many levels, suffers from this turning backwards towards the Old Testament, an age over 1500 years previous, with previous values. The gap between the artist's search for beauty and the subject matter, creates an unease. As a symbol of heroic Florence it also looked backwards: only a few years after Michelangelo carved the statue, Florence was conquered and lost its independence forever.

PONTORMO AND CÉZANNE

In painting Jacopo Pontormo (1494-1556) expresses this difficult dichotomy even better than Michelangelo – this search for a spiritual reality deeper than either the Church's dogma, or the obvious description of the exterior manifestations of nature.

Pontormo uses religious imagery to express the agitation and futurism of his own inner vision. His painting is no longer filled with natural space and light, but becomes again a flat surface covered in essentially abstract colours and forms. The primary object is not to imitate or describe nature, but to indicate through colour and shape, inner essences of nature, and thus to stimulate and reflect our feelings, to unite us all. Pontormo cuts deeply into reality – ours and the world's – to seek new truths. In many ways his work is one of the primary bases of modern art, and points directly to El Greco (1541-1614), to Goya (1746-1828), to Cézanne (1839-1906), to Van Gogh (1853-1890), and to Matisse (1869-1959).

The Renaissance could hardly go forward without giving up the ancient pan-European concept that Christianity should be directed and controlled through a powerful centralized bureaucracy. This concept of a single, all-powerful, temporal Church – a Christian Roman Empire – had lasted over a thousand years, from the time of the Roman Emperor Constantine in the 4th century A.D., when be made Christianity the religion of the Roman Empire.

Precisely because they abandoned that concept of the all-powerful Christian Church-Empire directed from Rome, it is in the liberal, trade dominated, Protestant countries that the Renaissance continued with the most vigour, rather than in the conservative Catholic ones.

In 1517, the originator of the Protestant Reformation, Luther, denied not Christ, but the temporal Church in Rome.

But it was only in the north of Europe where the power of the Roman Church was limited, that his message had lasting effect. In the south, the power of Spain, reinforced with the newly found gold of the New World, assured that the Roman Catholic Church remained dominant until the 19th century. Its power was finally broken by the conquests of Napoleon strangely enough, a man born in Corsica, but from an ancient Tuscan-Florentine family, the Buonaparte.

THE MEDICI AS POPES: 1513-1534

Soon after Lorenzo il Magnifico's death in 1492 the Medici family were expelled from Florence. This was the fault of Lorenzo's incompetent son, Piero (1471-1503), who alienated the Florentine people with his arrogant ways and weak government.

Caught between the family's banishment, failing finances, and an aggressive Church, the Medici changed sides. No longer significant traders, it was they who tipped the balance towards the Church, so that ecclesiastical power again predominated in Florence.

Lorenzo il Magnifico's son Giovanni (1475-1521), and his nephew, Giulio (1478-1534), became popes, the first as Leo X (1513-1521), the second as Clement VII (1523-1534). Because the sole sustaining wish of these two hardly religious prelates was to restore their family to power in Florence, they played Papal power-politics with France and Spain, finally convincing, after almost four decades of scandal and blood-letting, the latter to conquer the city for them.

This Spain accomplished decisively in 1530, duly establishing the Medici as the town's absolute rulers for the next 200 years, until the last Medici died in 1743. At the same time Spain became the dominant power in most of Italy until its conquest by Napoleon.

Both popes were, like almost all the Medici, exceptional patrons. But a sign of the times, a great deal of their patronage concerned Rome and the Church. Leo X employed Michelangelo in the construction of St. Peters, Raphael (1483-1520) in the decoration of the famous *Stanze* in the Vatican, and Leonardo to plan the draining of the Pontine Marshes. Clement VII was a patron of Leonardo, Cellini (1500-1571), and Raphael, as well as of Michelangelo, whom he employed in Florence to design the New Sacristy of San Lorenzo, and the Laurentian Library in the cloister attached to the Church.

AND THEN AS AUTHORITARIAN GRAND DUKES

After the restoration of the Medici as rulers of Florence by the Spanish in the 1530's, art reflected the significant economic and political changes which had taken place: the earlier Renaissance concerned itself with searching for truth;

Florentines, after the return of the Medici, were told what truth they were to believe. This can be clearly seen in the painting and sculpture of the period. It becomes preoccupied with technique, with style, with startling surface effects – with manner rather than meaning. How one said something became more important than what one said, sure sign of a decaying civilization. In Florence, the period is called after these manners, *Mannerist*.

For much of the rest of the 16th century and the early part of the 17th, Florence was mostly ruled by two powerful Grand Dukes, a papal title which Cosimo I had himself and his heirs given in 1569 by Pope Pius V.

Both these Medici – Cosimo I and Ferdinando I – were also remarkable patrons. For a city which knew its influence and independence were gone, at least the Medici managed to make Florentines think that their city was still an important place. Or perhaps they really only succeeded in persuading Florentines to forget how unimportant their glorious city had become...

COSIMO I (1519-1574)

Grand Duke Cosimo I was a cousin of Pope Clement VII, and was more a Medici than ever, being a descendant of both the first Cosimo, *Pater Patriae*, and of Cosimo's younger brother, Lorenzo.

Cosimo I ruled Florence with great energy for almost 40 years from 1537-1574, commissioning works on a scale which even the earlier Cosimo Pater Patriae would have appreciated. He extended his new home in Palazzo Pitti, and began to lay out the Boboli Garden behind it. In these he had theatrical evenings – *intermezzi* they were called – which were the beginnings of modern opera. He had Bartolomeo Ammannati (1511-1592) build the beautiful Ponte Santa Trinita, finish Michelangelo's Laurentian Library, as well as sculpt the enormous *Neptune* in Piazza Signoria, and design the lovely fountain around it. He was a patron of Bronzino (1503-1572), Pontormo, Cellini, Tribolo (1500-1550), Buontalenti (1536-1608), and of the northerner, Giambologna (1524-1608).

THE UFFIZI

Cosimo I also had Vasari build the Uffizi for him. Giorgio Vasari (1511-1574) was the many-talented Court architect of the moment, painter of the huge battle scenes in the Salone dei Cinquecento of Palazzo Vecchio, as well as the author of *The Lives of the Painters, Sculptors and Architects*, the first history of Italian art up to his day.

The building was begun in 1560, and completed in 1580 after Vasari's death. The word 'Uffizi' means 'the Offices', and Cosimo I's intention was to concentrate all the main municipal and regional offices, as well as the official workshops of the Medici Tuscan State, under one roof, attached by a corridor to Palazzo Vecchio, the seat of the government itself.

On the top floor of his 'Uffizi' building Cosimo I wished to display his collection of art. By the mid-16th century the Medici family had been the most important collectors and patrons in Florence – and even in Europe – for 150 years, some 6 generations, so there was already a vast collection.

Another corridor was built at the same time, in 1565, from the Uffizi along the river, across Ponte Vecchio, and on to Palazzo Pitti. This meant that Cosimo, his Court and his family could walk to and from work without having to descend into the street. The distancing of the Medici from the everyday life of their subjects, is another indication of the changes which took place in Florence in the 16th century. Cosimo I was no longer a man of the people, as had been the first Cosimo and Lorenzo il Magnifico. The new Cosimo was a ruthless dictator who's power was imposed by Spain, and by the Vatican in Rome.

It was at this time that the shops on Ponte Vecchio became dedicated to the sale of jewellery and gold. Previously butchers had traded on the bridge, so that waste could be easily disposed into the river, feeding the many fish that once swam there. Gold, of course, didn't smell as strongly as innards.

Today this corridor, which can be visited, is decorated with the a collection of self-portraits of artists.

From its inception until very recently the Uffizi building also housed all the City Records – the Archivio. These have now been moved, and the rooms which contained them are being adapted to the enlarged Uffizi Gallery planned for the future.

Cosimo I, followed by his sons Francesco I (1541-1587), and Ferdinando I (1549-1609), slowly brought together a great part of the artistic and scientific objects they owned. These filled first the lovely octagonal room called the *Tribuna*, and then the corridor which is now the entrance to the collection, still called the *Galleria delle Statue*, because of the many antique statues which were then put there.

The collections eventually filled both the long corridors of the top floor of the building, the short one joining them along the Arno, as well as all the rooms off them.

The vast section of drawings and engravings – one of the largest in the world – is kept in rooms below, rooms where once was the famous Medici Theatre, now no longer in existance.

The Uffizi collections originally included many things which have been moved to the Pitti, to the Bargello, the Accademia, the Museo Archeologico, the Science Museum, Palazzo Vecchio, and to other places.

The Pitti, in particular, being the main family residence from the 16th century onwards, still contains a large part of the collections, particularly of paintings. This was started in 1620 by Cosimo II (1590-1621).

It was Cosimo I and his son Francesco I, who had the ceilings of the entrance corridor of the Uffizi Gallery painted with the same sort of decoration which had been found on the walls and ceilings of ancient villas, dug up during the 16th century in Rome. Ferdinando I, Cosimo's last son, brought many antique sculptures from Villa Medici in Rome, and added armour and scientific instruments to the collections, as well. His grandson Ferdinando II (1610-1670) married a lady from Urbino, Vittoria della Rovere. She brought with her, either as dowry or inheritence, many wonderful things, including pictures by Raphael, and by Titian (1490-1576).

Cosimo III (1642-1723), who gave the Gallery a final basic arrangement it still has today, also added enormously to the collections, particularly things which had been gathered together by his learned uncle, Cardinal Leopoldo de' Medici (1617-1675).

Even after the last Medici died in 1743, the Lorraine family, which became the Grand Dukes of Tuscany in succession to the Medici, continued to add to the collections.

By the second half of the 19th century the collections had become so enormous and the Uffizi so overcrowded that a vast reorganization took place. This was after the unification of Italy. Tuscany had ceased to exist as a separate State.

Everything was grouped together logically, and housed in new quarters all over Florence. In the Uffizi itself remained the most important collection of pictures – particularly those from the 14th, 15th, and early 16th centuries – ancient statues, tapestries, and drawings, making the Gallery easily the most important museum of Florentine art in the world.

Since the 19th Century the collection has steadily and significantly increased. Today it is the one place where every moment of the whole extraordinary development of Florentine painting, through four centuries, is represented by a masterpiece. And because, too, of all the other non-Florentine pictures in the collection, the Uffizi is also one of the world's best general collections of paintings. In fact, together with those in Palazzo Pitti, and in the Vasarian Corridor which links the two collections physically, the three groups of pictures form the greatest collection of Renaissance and Italian post-Renaissance painting in existence.

FERDINANDO I (1549-1609) AND COSIMO II (1590-1621)

Grand Duke Cosimo's son Ferdinando I honoured his father by having Giambologna cast and erect the large equestrian portrait of him still standing in Piazza Signoria, and by continuing many of his father's numerous projects. He also organized the competition for the design of the *Cappella de' Principi*, the vast mausoleum in San Lorenzo, of inlaid marble, where many of the Medici are buried. Nothing expresses better that manner had triumphed over meaning, than a comparison of Michelangelo's sublime *Sagrestia Nuova* with the dubious taste of the nearby Capella de' Principi.

At the top of the Boboli Garden, overlooking the city, Ferdnando I built *Forte di Belvedere*, with its magnificent views. His son, Cosimo II, had the distinction of protecting Galileo (1564-1642) from the Papacy. Unfortunately the ruler died young, leaving a less enlightened successor. Galileo was soon tried before the Inquisition for telling the truth about the world – that it was moving – a phenomenon with which the anachronistic Vatican had more and more difficulty.

It was also at this time that the marvellous rooms in Palazzo Pitti which are now part of the *Museo degli Argenti* were frescoed (1635-1642) by Giovanni da San Giovanni, with helpers and pupils. They eulogize the Medici, who in allegory permit the ancient Muses, exiled from Parnassus, to settle in Tuscany.

THE LATER MEDICI

Remarkably adept at understanding the sources of political power, the Medici were first great traders, then wise rulers of Florence, then Popes – albeit hardly great ones.

Finally, after the Spanish had conquered Florence for them, and reinstalled them as Grand Dukes of Tuscany, they also began to understand that the real economic and political power in Europe lay more and more outside of Italy. It belonged to the large Nation States – France, Spain, Austria, England. So as Grand Dukes, the Medici allied themselves to these powers through marriage. Two became Queens of France: Catherine de' Medici in 1533, and Maria de' Medici in 1601. Of the many children of only these two marriages, two became Kings of France, two Queens of Spain, one Empress of Austria and two others Queens, respectively, of England, and of Scotland. Further Medici connections with, and influence upon, the ruling families of Europe through the children of those marriages, and through all their other marriages, was literally without end.

But Medici blood throughout the courts of Europe did not assure male heirs in Florence. Nor did that improve the Florentine economy, or revitalize the ever more decadent Medici family.

Florence in the following century went steadily downhill, while the Medici themselves became progressively less interested and less interesting.

By the end of the 1600's the whole Mediterranean world had become secondary. People of northern Europe had inherited the Renaissance. The search for truth about man and nature developed into modern science, modern agriculture, modern industry, and modern politics. During the late 1600's and early 1700's, Florence had little enough to do with those things. The city slowly lost its energy and its intellectual curiosity.

But the enormous legacy of profound thought through four centuries, from before the coining of the golden florin in 1252, until after the discoveries of Galileo in the 1600's – all that was absorbed into the mainstream of northern European thought, developed and passed on to our own time.

The major museums of the world are full of beautiful objects made in Florence during those four centuries – pictures, sculptures, furniture, coins and medals, jewellery, ceramics, weapons. Much too has been destroyed over the centuries, particularly things made in cloth, or of wood, glass, plaster, wax – or other perishable materials. Yet Florence today, with its incomparable churches still filled with sacred objects, with frescos, panel paintings, and sculpture, its palazzi, and fortresses, its bridges and its nearby villas, its gardens, its vistas, its magnificent public and private collections, its piazzas, its fountains, is still the only city-museum in the world.

Today, we are all descendants of those Florentine Renaissance ideas about human beings – about our great stature in nature and about our freedom to develop our own destiny. And still today, Florence belongs to all of us.

THE LAST MEDICI: ANNA MARIA LUISA DE' MEDICI GIVES ALL THE FAMILY COLLECTIONS TO THE PEOPLE OF FLORENCE – 1743

The last Medici was a woman. As Cosimo, Pater Patriae was the first great Medici patron, she was the last. And except for Cosimo, who started it all, she was perhaps the greatest patron of them all. She should really be called *Mater Patriae*, the mother of her country.

Although she hardly patronized artists or collections, it is because of her that we are still able to see and enjoy all the artistic objects the Medici put together. The last Grand Duke, Gastone de' Medici, died in 1737, without male heirs. His sister, Anna Maria Luisa (1667-1743), inherited the vast Medici moveable property – furniture and tapestries, coins and medals, antique statuary, archaelogical finds from all over the world, ceramics and porcelain, manuscripts, books, miniatures, paintings, drawings, prints, Renaissance statues and statuettes – the greatest private art collection the world had ever seen.

She willed that these collections were never to leave Florence. They were in effect to belong to the people of Florence, and were to be kept for the pleasure and benefit of the people of the whole world. This last gesture of the extraordinary Medici family gave to each one of us the contents of most of the wonderful museums in Florence today. Not only were they the greatest patrons and collectors of art in European history, the Medici were also the most generous. If Anna Maria Luisa had not written that will, it can be taken for granted that the enormous family collections would have been dispersed among the many Medici relatives all over Europe.

The end of the Renaissance

Although the Renaissance ended in Florence as the town lost its liberties, perhaps it didn't really end for the rest of Europe until the First World War.

It was only then the thin illusion that Europe was still Christian was forever discarded. Trade, and with it Science, finally triumphed. Before that traumatic war a Frenchman, an Englishman, a German – each would have claimed his country Christian. After the senseless killing during four insane years of millions of Christians by other Christians, the claim became meaningless: to love one's enemy is, after all, the bottom line of Christ's teaching.

Cézanne and a new Renaissance

Just as Giotto about the year 1300 showed the world both that the old order was finished, and what was coming, so did Cézanne 600 years later, in about 1900. Cézanne revivified Masaccio's image of Man dominant over nature, and integral with it. He tried to produce paintings in which Man was entirely at one with nature. The painter, his sitter, the landscape or still-life, the canvas, stretcher, and the colours themselves, were all parts of a whole, not so much reflections of nature, as all integrally part of it. Human beings, in particular, are of the same matter as everything else, not at all dominant over nature as they had taught themselves to think over so many centuries.

For Giotto's vision to blossom as it did years after his death, in the work of Masaccio, Donatello and Brunelleschi, all those dreadful decades of the 14th century – decades of economic depression, plague, death, war, social and religious upheaval – had to happen. The old world had to be destroyed to make space for the new, the old ideas and idols had to fall for there to be space for a new spirituality. Art grows naturally in that void where idols have died, from the unfettered love left behind.

THE FORMATION OF MODERN LIFE IN THIS CENTURY

The same has been true for Cézanne's vision. He died in 1906, and the 20th century was like the 14th, one of succeeding destructions of the old way of living: the First World War, the Depression, the Russian Revolution, civil war in Spain, the Second World War with its more than 20 million dead, wars of decolonization, concentration camps, purges, gulags, genocide and totalitarianism all over the globe, the Atomic Bomb, the Korean and Vietnam wars, and finally, as the new century and new Millenium begin, the threat of extinction through the over-population and irreversible polluting of the planet.

That old European male-dominated, world of racism, economic conquest, and exploitation, nationalism with its abetting churches – a world in which an arrogant pseudo-Christain man raped the world of its ancient cultures and its natural wealth, while pretending to do good by "Christianizing" it – had to pass.

It was essentially a self-destructive world, but we had to arrive at the Atomic Bomb to understand that. As in the 1420's man had reached a major moment in his development. After Hiroshima he could only go forwards. After Hiroshima the old world was gone forever.

OUR OWN RENAISSANCE

One hundred years passed between the time of Giotto in the early 14th century and that of Masaccio in the 15th. We are ourselves now one hundred years beyond the time of Cézanne. Trade in Florence and over much of the globe is today once again prosperous. No doubt there will be moments of regression, but trade, technology and ecology should lead us towards goals and towards a society which we can hardly imagine.

Previously it was the tension between the poles of Church and Trade which produced a Renaissance. Today it is a new tension which has already begun to produce our own New Age, our own Renaissance.

Every object we make, every significant action we take is now formed between those two poles of Technology and Ecology, and contains them both. Every automobile, every plastic bottle, every dam or autostrada is made with those two poles in mind – the shape, the size, the speed of the car is not limited by man's ingenuity, but by the practical considerations of the world in which it will move.

The pole of Technology is merely a development of the older faith in unrestrained, limitless Man and his Trade. Essentially it is materialistic faith. But the second – Ecology – is new, conservationist and clearly spiritual in its ideas and in its self-control, intent upon limiting technology – and thus materialism – to enhance life, to preserve the planet. Between their two positions a new tension is growing – just like that earlier one between Church and Trade – from whence will be formed Tomorrow, adapting itself to them both, but being neither.

Who, in this new world of ours, are the artistic heirs of Cézanne, the spokes-persons of our own Renaissance? Where are Masaccio, Donatello, Brunelleschi, Machiavelli, Leonardo, and Michelangelo? And what forms has their work taken, what forms will it take in the future?

While the Renaissance developed and then faded, the centers of Trade went first to northern Europe, and then to the New World, to New York and Chicago. Today trade flows freely over much of the globe, with many centers, none dominant. Perhaps as our new Renaissance develops the world will become what John Lennon hoped and sang for – One.

BIBLIOGRAPHY

ACTON, H., *The Last Medici*, London, 1932.

Burckhardt, J., *The Civilization of the Renaissance in Italy*, London, 1936.

CESATI, F., *The Medici*, Firenze, 1999.

CHEYNEY, E.P., *The Dawn of a New Era, 1250-1453*, New York, 1936.

CLASTER, J.N., *The Medieval Experience, 300-1400*, New York, 1982.

COCHRANE, E., *The Late Italian Renaissance*, New York, 1970.

FERGUSON, W.K., *Europe in Transition*, Boston, 1962.

FERGUSON, W.K., *Renaissance Studies*, University of Western Ontario, 1963.

GUTKIND, C.S., *Cosimo de' Medici, Pater Patriae, 1384-1464*, Oxford, 1938.

HALE, J.R., *Florence and the Medici*, London, 1977.

HAY, D., *The Italian Renaissance*, Cambridge (UK),1961

HAY, D., *The Medieval Centuries*, New York, 1964.

HEER, F.,*The Medieval World*, London, 1961.

HIBBERT, C., *The Rise and Fall of the House of Medici*, London, 1974.

HOLMES, G., *The Florentine Enlightenment, 1400-1450*, London, 1969.

HUIZINGA, J., *The Waning of the Middle Ages*, London, 1955.

JOHNSON, P., *The Renaissance*, London, 2000.

MEAD, R.D. (ed.), *Europe Reborn*, New York, 1975.

PIRENNE, H., *Economic and Social History of Medieval Europe*, London, 1936.

RUBINSTEIN, N., (ed.), *Florentine Studies: Politics and Society in Renaissance Florence*, London, 1968.

SCHEVILL, F., *The Medici*, New York, 1949.

SOUTHERN, R.W., *Western Society and the Church in the Middle Ages*, Harmondsworth, 1970.

SMITH, J. H., *The Great Schism*, London, 1970.

PLATES

1. *Inlay Florentine Lily* from the Cappella dei Principi in San Lorenzo, with the Ducal crown of the Medici encircling the middle petal. Stone inlay was a craft greatly encouraged by the Medici from the 16th century onwards. It is still practised in the city today.

2. *An Old map* showing the southern and eastern part of Tuscany, the land of the Etruscans. The northern boundary of Tuscany was originally the river Arno, or just north of it. The eastern and southern was the river Tiber, as can be clearly seen. Rome itself may have originally been an Etruscan town.

3. *The Coat of Arms of Fiesole,* in inlay marble from the Cappella dei Principi in San Lorenzo. Fiesole was founded in about 800 B.C., one of the twelve major Etruscan hill-towns. For some centuries Fiesole probably protected the smaller town of Florence below, an important crossing point on the Arno.

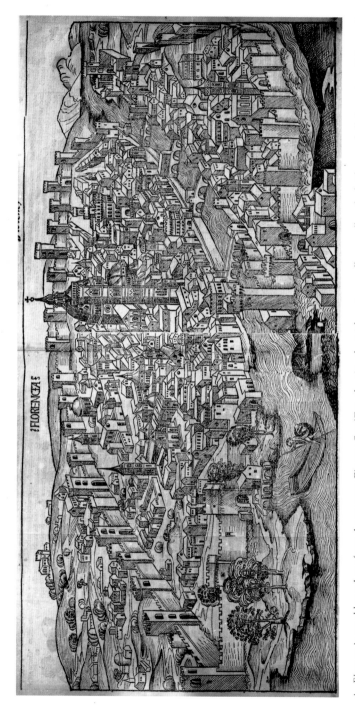

4. *Florence* in an old wood-cut from the museum Firenze Com'Era, showing the 14th century walls, as well as the bridges, and all the major religious and public buildings.

5. *Florence* in a 19th century water-colour in the museum Firenze Com'Era, by Emilio Burci, showing the apse of S. Croce, as well as the city walls on the north side of the river, pulled down in the second half of the 19th century.

6. *The Baptistry* in Florence. There have always been various opinions about the date of this wonderful building. It seems to have been built in the 8th or 9th century, but may well be much earlier, and may even be an early Christian building, on the site of a Roman temple.

7. *San Miniato al Monte*, the main altar. This marvellous church, with columns and pilasters which hark back to Roman times, was built in the 11th century. The mosaic of Christ in Glory, Saints John and Miniato, and the four Evangelists, dates from the late 13th century.

8. *Or San Michele,* a detail of the floor mosaics. Abstract patterns continue to appear in Florentine art from the earliest times right through the Renaissance. This is a *mandala*: a square, symbolizing the earth, contains a circle, a symbol of continuity and life. The circle contains the star of 64 parts formed into pyramids, leading inwards to a point—infinity.

9. *Detail of an Old Map of Florence.* The original Roman grid-pattern to the streets of the town centre is quite clear, as is the oval site of the Roman amphitheatre, on the left.

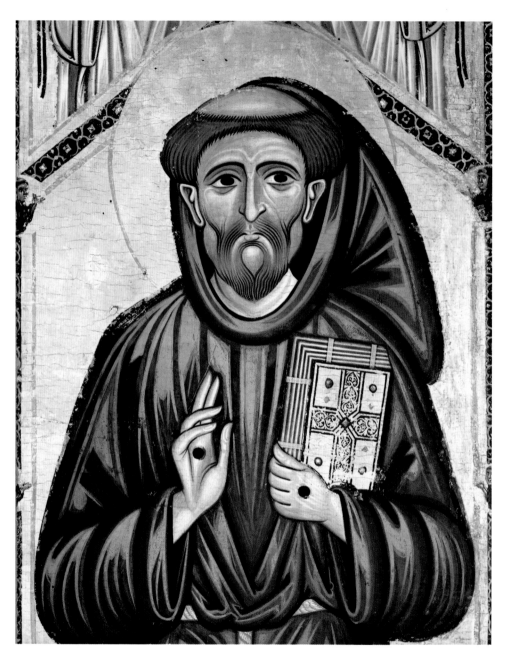

10. *St Francis,* detail of a painting in Santa Croce, probably by the Master of Vico l'Abbate, ca. 1250. Saints Francis and Dominic were the two most prominent of scores of church reformers who appeared from early Christian times onward. Almost all of them preached poverty and a return to the spirit of Christ and of early Christianity. Preaching by Saints Francis and Dominic caused the beginning of a social revolution which eventually made ordinary Christians as important or even, in some sects of Christianity, more important, than priests.

11. *Santa Croce,* in Florence. A vast Franciscan complex, the second largest in the world after their church at Assisi, this was built in the 14th century. Besides religious responsibilities, the friars provided society with every social need from health assistance to shelter for the poor, to elementary and trade schools, to job placement – all the things the State does today were earlier in the care of the various religious orders.

12. *Fresco* of the great Dominican saint, Thomas Aquinas enthroned, at his feet three major heretics, and at his sides major doctors of the Old and New Testament, in the cloister at Santa Maria Novella, by Andrea da Firenze ca. 1355. Below are the sciences and arts personified by seated female figures, with their major representatives seated at their feet. Saints Francis and Dominic formed orders of monks devoted to poverty. But these orders, which were an attempt to return Christianity to its original principles, were so successful that they soon became the largest and richest, building new churches in every major town in Europe.

13. *Santa Maria Novella,* in Florence. Built in an Italian Gothic style in the 14th century, this beautiful church was the home of monks belonging to the Dominican order, followers of St Dominic. Their symbol is the barking dog. The word *Dominican* was seen as a combination of the word *domini* – "of the Lord" – and *cani,* "dogs": Dogs of the Lord. The Dominicans are an order of preachers.

14. *The Gold Florin* became the dollar of its day, a universal currency in Europe. It was first minted in Florence in 1252. This one is now in the Bargello.

15. *Portrait Cameo of Cosimo Medici, Pater Patriae.* In keeping with the modesty of this extraordinary man who was the first catalyst of the Renaissance in Florence, there are few portraits of Cosimo il Vecchio taken in his life-time. This is probably a copy done in the later 15th century.

16. *Ponte Vecchio*, a photograph from before the destructions of the city on both banks of the river during World War II. The bridge was re-built after the flood of 1333 had destroyed its predecessor. It has survived many floods over the last five-and-one-half centuries, including that of 1966. The corridor leading across the bridge, by which the Medici were able to go from Palazzo Vecchio and the Uffizi, to Palazzo Pitti, is clearly visible.

17. *Madonna and Child,* painted by Giotto in about 1310 for the church of Ognissanti, now in the Uffizi. Giotto, Masaccio, and Michelangelo are the three great names in Florentine painting: Giotto in the 14th century indicated that man exists in space; Masaccio in the 15th, made man the principal actor on the world's stage, and gave the stage natural space and light; Michelangelo, in the 16th, made man into an unnatural superman while destroying the natural space which made him earth-bound.

18. *A Sculptor at Work*. A relief by Andrea Pisano from the Cathedral Bell-tower, now in the Museo dell'Opera del Duomo, first-half of the 14th century. During the Middle Ages sculpture was a much more important art than painting. The situation changed dramatically in the 14th and 15th centuries in Italy, partly due to the influence of the Franciscan and Dominican orders, preaching poverty. Paintings cost little – much less than sculpture – just the price of colours and the suface to paint upon.

19. *The Beheading of St John the Baptist,* one of the scenes on the south doors of the Baptistry, by Andrea Pisano, sculpted in about 1330. Originally these doors faced the Cathedral. They were displaced by Ghiberti's second pair of doors, (fig. 39), called by Michelangelo, the "Gates of Paradise". Although Ghiberti's work is more technically brilliant than that of Andrea Pisano, in some ways the concentrated poignancy of these scenes is artistically superior.

20. *The Tomb of John XXIII* (d. 1419). John XXIII was one of a series of popes and anti-popes, during the Great Schism, 1378-1417. He appointed the Medici to the position of Pope's bankers, assuring them thus great wealth and power. The large tomb by Donatello and Michelozzo, is placed unusually in the church dedicated to re-birth – the Baptistry. So it is not only a symbol of the re-birth of the church, but also, in its classical style with Roman lettering, of re-birth in art. Its great size also symbolizes the debt of thanks the Medici owed the Pope.

21. *Pope Martin V,* by Jacopino da Tradate, in Milan's Cathedral. Probably sculpted in 1418 at the time of Martin's passage through Milan, the figure is of the Pope who re-established the Church's power in Italy and in Europe generally, after the Great Schism. He was a Roman of the Colonna family. His symbol, a column, is on the base of his throne.

22. *Detail of St Peter Enthroned,* by Masaccio, in the Brancacci Chapel, Santa Maria del Carmine, Florence, painted about 1425. St Peter is shown enthroned without the traditional symbols of Papal authority – elegant robes, the Papal crown, and the keys of heaven (see fig. 21). He's also shown praying, rather than displaying papal power.

23. *The Trinity,* by Masaccio, ca. 1425, in Santa Maria Novella, Florence. This strange painting pictures Christ as an ordinary human being, crucified, his cross uplifted by God the Father, in a gesture similar to that of the priest lifting up the bread wafer in the mass, which took place on the altar, below. Although the painting is called *The Trinity,* it's really about man: not only is Christ an ordinary man, but Mary, on the left, and St John on the right are also ordinary people. So are the two donors, outside the Sepulchre. Besides, the painting is about man-made, magnificent, classical architecture, as well as about perspective, light, and natural space. Just as God the Father formed the world, so, too, is man able to idealize it.

24. *The Tribute Money,* detail, by Masaccio, ca. 1425, in the Cappella Brancacci, Santa Maria del Carmine, Florence. The painter modelled his figures on ancient statues (see fig. 25), and placed them in a natural world of space, air and light. The colour composition of these cloaks, is one of the great abstract compositions of Renaissance art, echoing the energy rhythms of music.

25. *Roman High-relief Sculpture,* on the arch at Beneventum, east of Naples. Masaccio studied the statuesque in ancient art such as this, to give his paintings a sculptural and classical quality. This re-birth of the study of the ancient world was one of the principal ingredients of the Renaissance.

26. *Detail from St Peter Enthroned,* by Masaccio, in the Cappella Brancacci, Santa Maria del Carmine, Florence (see fig. 22). This may be a self-portrait of the artist. The head on the left may be that of Masolino, who also worked in the Chapel. If this is, in fact, Masaccio's self-portrait, it is significant that he looks not at the pope enthroned, but at us. It is also probably the firts major self-portrait of a painter in the Florentine Renaissance.

27. *St George,* by Donatello, 1416. This figure, now in the Bargello, was
originally made for one of the 14 niches placed on the exterior of the church of
Or San Michele, each one dedicated by a Guild. St George was the patron of
the armorers. In the Middle Ages statues were normally conceived as part of
architecture. The statuary on Or San Michele, however, was different, conceived quite separately from the architecture. It is also remarkably humanistic.

28. *St Thomas' Doubt,* Or San Michele, by Verrocchio, 1466-83. The difference between the Gothic architecture of the building built a whole century before, and this Renaissance niche, is striking. Verrocchio solved the problem of fitting two figures into the restricted space by placing one outside the niche.

29. *The Cupola of Florence's Cathedral*, 1420-36. Filippo Brunelleschi built this enormous structure without using scaffolding, a perfect octagonal Renaissance structure placed on top of a Gothic one below. A view of the Church as planned, with a much smaller Gothic dome, exists in a fresco in the chapter-room of Santa Maria Novella.

30. *The Battle of San Romano*, central picture of three by Paolo Uccello, ca. 1456, Florence, Uffizi. The other two are in the Louvre, in Paris, and the National Gallery, London. The Renaissance brought a new way of looking at the world. Here Uccello reduces the turbulent battle scene to clustered abstract forms, while bringing the steep background hill forward, an almost flat plane covered with wonderful patterns. The lines of the lances serve to suggest the tension and careful underlying mathematics.

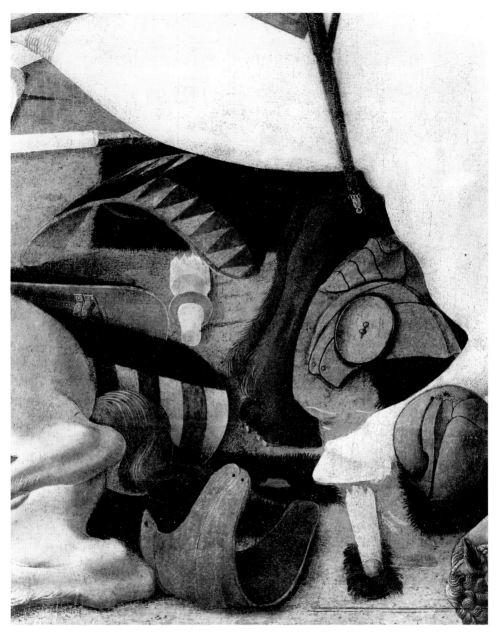

31. *A Detail from Uccello's Battle of San Romano* (fig. 30), not unlike a cubist painting of this century. Masaccio's development of painting released arists to search out new forms in nature, without many of the earlier religious prejudices.

32. *Madonna and Child* by Filippo Lippi, ca. 1465, Florence, Uffizi. Lippi was another artist who searched deeply for new visual forms in painting. Without the halos, and the pious attitudes of the Virgin and her Child, this painting becomes an elegant portrait. The background can be seen either as a painting itself, or as a view through a window – giving the picture a sense of unreality. Lippi's frescos in the Cathedral at Prato, near Florence, are among the finest paintings made during the whole Renaissance.

33. *The Last Supper,* by Andrea del Castagno, ca. 1450, Sant'Apollonia, Florence. This is another example of the rich search for abstract forms in painting which went on in post-Masaccio Florentine art. The figures of the Apostles themselves are quite unreal, reduced to a group of serious, heavily-robed, male figures. While the roof, the ceiling, the frieze, the white strip of the table cloth, the pilasters, the extraordinary floor – like some piece of modern kinetic art – each is an exceptional painting in itself, quite detached from the Apostles. The six marble panels behind the heads of the Apostles are so similar to modern abstract canvases as to be uncanny.

34. *Detail of fig. 33.* The parallels with modern art are remarkable.

35. *Palazzo Medici-Riccardi,* built by Michelozzo Michelozzi, 1444-60, for Cosimo il Vecchio. The building was originally smaller, having only one principal door and two ground-floor openings on its front. About it Cosimo is supposed to have lamented, "Such a large house for such a small family" ... The Medici were to build many more Tuscan homes over the next three centuries, besides marrying into all the greatest palaces of Europe.

36. *Interior Courtyard of Palazzo Medici*, showing their crest of balls, over the central arch. The word Medici means "doctors" and the balls may have originally been pills, as it was usual to put what was traded on a shield. Balls could also have referred to their trade as bankers – gold balls are still today the symbol of pawnbrokers.

37. *The Arrival of the Magi at Bethlehem*, by Benozzo Gozzoli, ca. 1459-60, detail from the mural decorations in the private family chapel in Palazzo Medici. The painter uses a religious theme to paint portraits of many of the important people in Florence in the middle of the 15th century. The strong tendency of Florentine art towards abstraction can be seen in the treatment of foliage and rock behind the heads of the figures.

38. *Castello di Trebbio*, in the Mugello, north of Florence. Built by Michelozzo in about 1460 for Cosimo il Vecchio and his family as a sort of hill-top mediaeval *castello*. Very likely it was used for hawking. Amerigo Vespucci, who was a Medici employee, and for whom America is named, lived here as a young man.

39. *The East Doors of the Baptistry,* Florence, Lorenzo Ghiberti, (1425-52), called the "Gates of Paradise" by Michelangelo. The ten scenes from episodes in the Bible are sculpted and cast with a fineness rarely equalled in art, combined into an architectonic structure of the same high quality. This is the "re-birth" of art, which the artists of the Renaissance wanted so earnestly to accomplish.

40. *Bust of an Unknown Lady,* by Desiderio da Settignano, ca. 1460. Humanism meant among other things that ordinary people, rather than past religious figures, became the main object of attention in life. This magnificent portrait bust shows once again how the Florentines managed to reduce reality to the simplest abstract forms.

41. *Prudence,* San Miniato al Monte, Florence, by Luca della Robbia, ca. 1465. Even the art of ceramics, so difficult to use for artistic expression, was carried to the level of a great art, by Luca della Robbia.

42. *San Lorenzo,* by Filippo Brunelleschi, 1420-60. This was the family church of the Medici. Its bare facade contrasts with the elegant, logical, light-filled interior. Various projects were made for facing the front of the building, including one by Michelangelo, but none of them ever came about.

43. *San Lorenzo,* detail of the interior. Brunelleschi revolutionized the religious architecture of the time, by making it spacious, logical, and light-filled – more a product of the mind than of the emotions. This is a reflection of the independent attitude towards Christianity and the Papacy in Rome, which came about in Florence during and after the Great Schism.

44. *The Library at San Marco,* by Michelozzo, 1444. Cosimo Medici, the grandfather of Lorenzo il Magnifico, was not only the greatest patron of his day, and maybe the greatest in all European history, he was also the greatest bibliophile. He had Michelozzo build this magnificent library for the monastery at San Marco.

45. *Niccolò Machiavelli*, a posthumous portrait in Palazzo Vecchio, by Santi di Tito (1536-1603). Machiavelli was one of the most interesting figures in the Florentine Renaissance, and one of the greatest political thinkers ever. His *Discourses* are full of pithy wisdom. Machiavelli felt that Italy could never unify itself to become once again a modern and great nation, as long as the Church in Rome existed as a temporal power.

46. *Lorenzo de Medici,* called Il Magnifico (1448-1492). A portrait cameo now in the Museo degli Argenti, in Florence. Lorenzo ruled over Florence from 1464 to 1492, from the death of his father Piero the Gouty, to his own early death aged 44. Already, during his years as ruler the seed of Florence's demise as a free city had been planted in its economic decline.

47. *The Birth of Venus* and *The Return of Spring* (fig. 48), by Sandro Botticelli, (1445-1510), both in the Uffizi, Florence. During the second half of the 15th century in Florence, thinkers tried to reconcile Greek philosophy – particularly that of Plato – with contemporary Christian ideas. Both these pictures were painted for a cousin of Lorenzo il Magnifico, also called Lorenzo, and attempt that reconciliation. Both depict the two forms of beauty in Plato's symposium: heavenly beauty, and natural beauty. *The Birth of Venus*: Venus is a symbol of Divine Love. She is seen born of the sea, fathered by Uranus – who is symbolized by the foam under her shell. Her birth is also her arrival in the natural world, symbolized by Flora, who welcomes her to the shore.

48. In *The Return of Spring*, Venus represents the union of Divine and Natural Love. The three figures to the right are Zephyr, the wind, and his wife Chloris; their union produces Flora (the third figure from the right), who is Nature. On the far left is Mercury, who personifies Reason, and the three graces, Beauty. Venus, is the last and central figure. She, with a halo of leaves and light, represents Human Love as well as Man's Soul. Through the contemplation of Natural Reason and Natural Beauty, and through the grace of Divine Love (symbolized by Cupid and his arrow above), man's soul is able to attain God, indicated by Mercury's baton pointing skyward.

49. *Madonna and Child with the Infant St John, St Martin, St Catherine, and Two Donors*, by Filippino Lippi (1457-1504), in Santo Spirito. Filippino was the son of Fra Filippo Lippi and his mistress, a nun, Lucrezia Buti. Mother and son appear as Madonna and Child in many of the older Lippi's works. This picture, painted as the end of the 15th century, just as Florence was about to lose its long-treasured liberty, still retains much of the calm which Florence experienced during Lorenzo il Magnifico's time.

QVI
DOVE CON I SVOI
CONFRATELLI FRA DOMENICO
BVONVICINI E FRA SILVESTRO
MARVFFI IL XXIII MAGGIO
DEL MCCCCXCVIII PER INIQVA
SENTENZA FV IMPICCATO ED ARSO
FRA GIROLAMO SAVONAROLA
DOPO QVATTRO SECOLI
FV COLLOCATA QVESTA
MEMORIA

50. *A Plaque* marking where Savonarola died, in Piazza della Signoria. By having Savonarola burned in 1498, the Papacy reclaimed a power over Florence it had lost at the time of the Great Schism more than a hundred years before, or even earlier.

51. *Michelangelo,* on a medal by Leoni Leone (1509-92) now in the Bargello. Michelangelo's task of portraying Christians as supermen, or even as good, in an Age that was often not so Christian nor so good, left much of his work with an unsettled, worried character.

52. *Tomb of Lorenzo, Duke of Urbino, in the Sagrestia Nuova*, S. Lorenzo, by Michelangelo, ca. 1521-26. The attempt to reconcile Christian ideals with pagan ones is particularly poignant in Michelangelo's work. Here there is not a vestige of Christianity at all – and yet the monument is purportedly a Christian tomb.

53. *Tomb of Cosimo II* in the Cappella dei Principi, San Lorenzo. The chapel was begun in the 17th century by Matteo Nigretti (d. 1649). The bronze statue is the work of Ferdinando Tacca (1616/19-1686). A harsh difference in artistic merit between the Sagrestia Nuova and Medici Mausoleum reflects the sad spiritual fortunes of Florence between the 1520's and a century later.

54. *Leo X, with Cardinals Giulio de Medici and Luigi de Rossi,* by Raphael, ca. 1518, in the Uffizi. The Medici
had been important bankers during the 15th century, particularly for the Papacy. In the 16th century, with the
decline in Florence's and their own fortunes, they became Popes. Leo X (1513-21) was one of Lorenzo il
Magnifico's children, and his nephew, Giulio, the left-hand figure in this painting, became Pope Clement VII
(1523-34). As Popes, the Medici continued their extraordinary history of patronage.

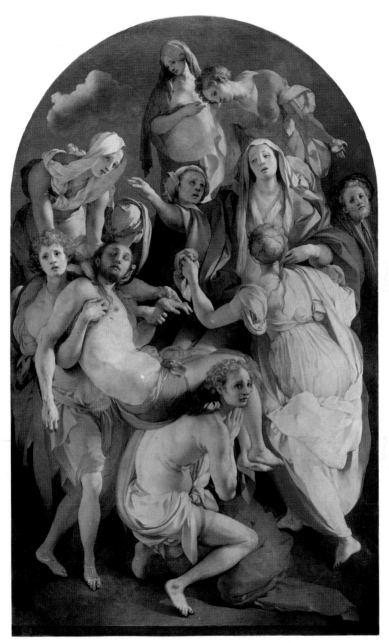

55. *The Deposition, by Jacopo Pontormo* (1494-1556). Aside from the desperate faces of the protagonists, this painting (1526-28) is a large abstract composition of many shapes and intriguing colours: much bunched and crinkled cloth, bare skin, foreshortened limbs, voids. The center is an empty space above Christ's legs. Even Christ's body seems light on the tip-toes of the figures below. Pontormo plants a post-Renaissance seed for painting which eventually flowers in the modern world.

56. *An Old Zocchi print of Ponte a Santa Trinita*, 18th century. The bridge was built by Bartolomeo Ammannati (1511-92). Michelangelo may have helped Ammannati with its design (1567-69), although the bridge was actually built after Michelangelo's death. It was among the last of Cosimo I's many projects in Florence.

57. *The Uffizi and Palazzo Vecchio.* Cosimo I (1519-1574) had Giorgio Vasari (1511-74) build the Uffizi (1559-80), and then join it with corridors both to Palazzo Vecchio and, by means of a corridor over the Ponte Vecchio (see fig. 16) to Palazzo Pitti. The word 'Uffizi' means 'Offices'. Cosimo I wanted the city's main administrative offices all under one roof. He also wanted space to display the Medici art collections. This could hardly be done during his own life time, as the building was only completed at the time of his death. But his successors slowly extended the top floor galleries so that they could house much of the family collection.

58. *Cosimo I,* by Benvenuto Cellini (1500-1571). Cosimo Medici, the first Grand Duke, was almost as energetic and accomplished a patron of the arts as his namesake Cosimo il Vecchio. Still today, all over Florence, there are works instigated by him. This magnificent bust was made in two parts between 1546 and 1557.

59. *Ceiling Decoration.* The Uffizi Gallery was decorated with motifs similar to this one, which imitated the decorations in ancient Roman villas, dug up during the 16th century.

60. *Portrait of Lucrezia Panciatichi,* ca. 1540, by Agnolo Bronzino (1503-72), in the Uffizi. In the 16th century Florence became preoccupied with external effects – with manners – rather than with inner meanings. Hence the term "Mannerism" used for art of the period. This highly polished portrait, technically quite extraordinary, exemplifies the taste of the time. Bronzino was essentially Court Painter to the Medici.

61. *Map of Florence in mid-16th century.* This was Florence at the time of Cosimo I. The massive Fortezza da Basso (1534-35) has been built into the city walls (to the west), but the Forte di Belvedere (1590-95),with its marvellous views of the city, has not. Palazzo Pitti, and the Boboli Garden behind, can be discerned. As can the enormous religious complexes – Santa Croce, Sant'Agostino, Santo Spirito, Santa Maria del Carmine, Santa Maria Novella, San Lorenzo, San Marco, Santissima Annunziata, as well as San Salvatore and San Miniato, outside the walls.

62. *Palazzo Pitti,* in an 18th century engraving by Cosimo Zocchi. Although the Medici family lived in Palazzo Pitti from the 16th to the mid-18th centuries, the building always retained its original name, for the family which began it in about 1460. Enlarged in the 1560's and in the 1640's, it was brought to its present form in the late 18th and early 19th centuries. For a time Palazzo Pitti was the largest private home in Europe.

63. *The Amphitheatre* in the Boboli Garden behind Palazzo Pitti, seen from the second floor of the building, with Forte di Belvedere behind. Imitative of the circuses of ancient Rome, this open-air stage with six rows of benches on three sides, was built by the Medici for their more extravagant spectacles (see fig. 64). The granite tub in the center came from the Baths of Caracalla in Rome; the obelisk from Luxor in ancient Egypt. The Boboli Garden was originally planned in about 1550 by the wife of Cosimo I, Eleanor of Toledo. It is among the largest and finest of all Italian gardens.

64. *The Amphitheatre* behind Palazzo Pitti in an old engraving. The occasion is a 17th century Medici wedding. The scene: "Hercules accompanied by carriages of the Sun and the Moon, is followed by Knights from Europe, America and Asia".

65. *The Neptune Fountain* in Piazza Signoria (ca. 1565-75), by Bartolomeo Ammannati (1511-92). This consists of four horses and three tritons around the giant Neptune. Twelve bronze figures are placed at the corners of the water basin. The fountain was commissioned by Cosimo I as a reference to his dream that Florence become a great sea-power. Florentines have always referred to it irreverently as, "Il Biancone" – "The Big White Thing". Now, apparently through poor restoration, the legs of Neptune are yellow: Florentines call him *Il Giallone* – «The Big Yellow Thing»...

66. *Honour Triumphant Over Falsehood* (1570), by Vincenzo Danti (1530-76), now in the Bargello. Danti was one of the sculptors who worked in Michelangelo's shadow, a fine craftsman but without the intellectual force of the great master. He also lived in a time which required of Florentine artists praise of Medici rule, rather than expression of original, searching ideas.

67. *Detail of a Fresco of the Muses Arriving in Tuscany,* by Cecco Bravo (?-1661). Part of a sumptuous decoration eulogizing Lorenzo il Magnifico in Palazzo Pitti. These were commissioned to celebrate the marriage of Ferdinando II with Vittoria della Rovere, and were painted about 1635-40.

68. *Cosimo II (1590-1621) with his wife Maria Maddalena d'Austria, and his brother Francesco,* by Justus Sustermans (1597-1681). Except for his protection of Galileo (1564-1642) Cosimo II accomplished little in his short life. The Medici family and Duchy were in a slow decline which lasted just over a further hundred years, until the eclipse of the family in 1743.

ANNA MARIA LVDOVICA
COSMI III·M·E·DVCIS FILIA IOHANNIS GV⁄I:
LELMI COMITIS PALAT·RHENI ET ELECT·VXOR

69. *Anna Maria Ludovica de Medici* (1667-1743), the last of the family, in an old engraving. It was she who left all the collections of the Medici in such a way that they essentially belonged forever to the people of the city of Florence.

70. *The Medici Balls,* on the base of a statue of Giovanni delle Bande Nere de Medici (1498-1526), the father of Cosimo I, by Baccio Bandinelli (1488-1560), now in Piazza San Lorenzo.

FINITO DI STAMPARE
NELLA TIPOGRAFIA GIUNTINA
FIRENZE - FEBBRAIO 2001

POCKET LIBRARY OF STUDIES IN ART

20. Jürgen Paul, *Der Palazzo Vecchio in Florenz. Ursprung und Bedeutung seiner Form.* 1969, 96 pp. con 41 ill. f.t.

21. Margherita Gabrielli, *Il ciclo francescano di Assisi. Considerazioni stilistiche e storico-teologiche.* 1970, 120 pp. con 41 ill. n.t.

22. Richard Fremantle, *Florentine Painting in the Uffizi. An Introduction to the historical Background.* 1971, VI-172 pp. con 64 ill. n.t.

23. Mauro Cristofani, *Introduzione allo studio dell'Etrusco.* 1973, VIII-200 pp. con ill. n.t. e 1 tav. f.t. Ristampa 1997.

24. Edgar Hertlein, *Masaccios Trinität. Kunst, Geschichte und Politik der Frührenaissance in Florenz.* 1979, XIV-270 pp. con 79 ill. f.t.

25. Edward G. Clare, *St. Nicholas: His legends and iconography.* 1985, 112 pp. con 64 ill. n.t.

26. Luba Freedman, *Titian's Independent Self-Portraits.* 1990, 128 pp. con 35 ill. n.t.

27. Richard Fremantle, *God and Money. Florence and the Medici in the Renaissance. Including Cosimo I's Uffizi and its Collections.* 1992, 62 pp. con 70 tavv. f.t. Ristampa 2001.

28. Oscar Mandel, *The art of Alessandro Magnasco: an essay in the recovery of meaning. With a survey of Magnasco paintings in North American public collections by Elizabeth Howard.* 1994, 214 pp. con 14 ill. in nero f.t. e 1 tavola a colori.

29. Katerine Gaja, *G. F. Watts in Italy. A portrait of the artist as a young man.* 1995, 152 pp. con 70 ill. n.t. di cui 9 a colori.

30. Giovan Battista Fidanza, *Vincenzo Danti 1530-1576.* 1996, 134 pp. con 37 ill. f.t.

31. Pierpaolo Luderin, *L'Art* pompier. *Immagini, significati, presenze dell'altro Ottocento francese (1860-1890).* 1997, 196 pp. con 134 ill. f.t.

32. Ginevra Tomasi, *I bronzi decorativi del mobile Impero in Toscana. Le tecniche e gli artisti.* 1999, VI-218 pp. con 13 ill. n.t. e 42 f.t.

33. Katherine T. Brown, *The Painters Reflection. Self-Portraiture in Renaissance Venice.* In preparazione.

34. Gigetta Dalli Regoli, *Il gesto e la mano. Convenzione e invenzione nel linguaggio figurativo fra Medioevo e Rinascimento.* 2000, 88 pp. con 172 ill. f.t. di cui 8 a colori.